To: Bert & Helga Berrang

Mery Christmas
Covenant Church

THE CHALLENGE TO CARE

The Challenge to Care

Charles Simpson

Servant Publications
Ann Arbor, Michigan

Copyright © 1986 by Charles Simpson
All rights reserved.

Cover design by Charles Piccirilli, Graphicus Corp.

Vine Books is an imprint of Servant Publications especially designed to serve Evangelical Christians.

Published by Servant Books
P.O. Box 8617
Ann Arbor, Michigan 48107

Printed in the United States of America
ISBN 0-89283-269-X

This book is dedicated to my father, who was my pastor and who taught me to care for God's people, and to all men and women who give their lives to caring for God's people.

In addition, I dedicate this effort to Don Basham, Ern Baxter, Bob Mumford, Derek Prince, and Ken Sumrall, who in many ways have helped me define what it means to care.

Finally, I must express my gratitude to my secretaries and typists, Connie Malkin, Kathy Tyrrell, Susan Hightower, and Sherry Tiedemann, and to Kevin Perrotta and the staff at Servant Books, whose hours of patient labor made this book possible.

Contents

Introduction/ix

I: *Pastoring as Personal Care*/1
1. Pastor and Son of a Pastor/3
2. Something More/9
3. ... and Fire/15
4. Pastoring People/21
5. Extending the Chief Shepherd's Care/27

II: *Who Is Qualified?*/33
6. Call/35
7. Character/41
8. Capacities/49
9. Spiritual Gifting/55

III: *Developing New Leaders*/63
10. The Process/65
11. Recognition/71

IV: *Real Leadership*/77
12. "The Shoot Out" over Authority/79
13. Strong or Weak Pastoral Leaders?/85

V: *Disciple-Making*/93
14. Who Should Make Disciples?/95
15. How Discipleship Happens/103
16. Advice and Cautions/113

VI: *Care Groups*/119
    17. Why Have Small Groups in the Church?/121
    18. Making Care Groups Work/125

VII: *Goals of Pastoral Ministry*/131
    19. Determining Our Direction/133
    20. People Goals/139
    21. Church Goals/145
    22. World Goals/155

VIII: *Pastors Relate to Other Pastors*/159
    23. Standing Together/161
    24. Pastoral Ethics/171

Conclusion/179

Introduction

NOT VERY LONG AGO dimes, quarters, half dollars, and even dollars were made out of silver. Now most of our coins are silver-coated copper. I recently bought a real silver dollar for my son, who collects coins; I paid twenty-two dollars for it. Words are like coins; they can lose their content and therefore lose their value. The form is there, but the substance has changed. We may never again see our coins minted in silver, but we can restore substance to words.

The English language is blessed to have been a vehicle for various translations of Holy Scripture. The Bible gives a certain permanent substance to various words. I have in my possession an 1828 Noah Webster Dictionary. I am impressed by how often Webster goes back to the Bible to define words. In fact, the first edition of Noah Webster's Dictionary has been reprinted to restore some of the original substance to American use of the English language. In a far greater way, the Bible "keeps the silver in our coins."

It is in that spirit that I want to present this treatise on the oft-used word, Pastor. I have a special love for the term and those whom it describes. It is my hope that they will be encouraged "to keep the silver in the coin."

The entire church has a stake in the matter. The pastor is but a symbol of what the entire church should be. The attributes and activities put forward here will be more than a single individual can accomplish. It will be my purpose to set forth the pastoral ministry in such a way that we can see the entire church participating in the challenge to care.

I much prefer to deal with positive definition and purpose. But it is also necessary to warn of various pitfalls and misconceptions—some that I have learned out of personal experience. I will, therefore, point out some problem areas.

My perspective is shaped by a particular background. At this writing, my father is still actively pastoring after more than fifty years. Most of those years were in a single Southern Baptist church. I have pastored since 1957, the time divided between Southern Baptist and nondenominational pastorates. But I have been privileged to minister in most of the major denominations and to sit in many conferences with pastors of various backgrounds. My observation is that pastoral challenges are much the same everywhere.

I write as one member of the fraternity to others. This is one man's view which, I trust, will stir us all to better understand our calling.

I will try to be biblical because I was trained to see the Bible as my source of authority in faith and practice. I will also try to be practical because our challenges are not merely theoretical—they are real. Here is praying that I can contribute to the success of all those who carry pastoral responsibilities, great or small, and thereby to the church of Jesus Christ.

Part I:
Pastoring As Personal Care

ONE

Pastor and Son of a Pastor

THE BIBLE IS A BOOK ABOUT GOD and how he has revealed himself through the lives of people. God is constantly working truth in human experience. God does not allow truth to remain abstract or isolated from the everyday realities of ordinary people. His love constantly confronts us with truth.

Because the revelation of God comes through human experience, personal experience is a legitimate way to talk about truth. The truths about exercising care for God's people cannot be isolated from personal challenges in real situations.

I find it natural to talk about my own pastoral convictions by reference to the situations in which God has spoken to me. For that reason this book will tell some of my personal story.

I was born into some serious convictions about Christianity in general and pastoring in particular. Grandpa Simpson was a deacon for forty years in an Alabama Baptist church. Dad dropped out of college in the Depression and got a job in New Orleans, where he attended what later became known as New Orleans Baptist Theological Seminary. While in New Orleans, Dad became involved in a local church that was establishing mission stations deep in the bayous of south Louisiana. Mom was converted along with her family under my Dad's ministry. After marriage, she joined my Dad in a strong commitment to Christian service. They lived and ministered without a regular salary, trusting God to supply, as they built small churches and prayer groups along the bayous. I was born into that family in 1937.

Growing up, my idea of a pastor was of a young, fiery preacher who often wept when he prayed, preached loudly, and shook everybody's hand when they left the meeting place. He was the main man. He knew everybody, and they knew him. He told people what God said and what they ought to do. A pastor was busy most of the time, visiting people, conducting meetings, and solving problems—especially solving problems.

When I was six our family moved to a small town in south Alabama near Mobile, and when I was fourteen years old I made a clear personal commitment to Jesus Christ. I had earlier joined the church at the age of twelve but had not achieved peace with God. I was old enough both to enjoy sin and be miserable in it. One night after a church service I prayed with an evangelist who was conducting services at our church. My prayer was simple: "Lord, I cannot be a Christian. I have tried and I cannot. If I am ever going to be one, you will have to do it." I had the distinct sense that he had been waiting for me to say that and that he would do it. I found peace with God through Jesus Christ and the power of the Holy Spirit.

Becoming a Christian was a difficult decision, but not nearly as difficult as deciding to be a minister. By the time I was seventeen, I had become a rather cool Christian—"duck tails," penny loafers, white tee shirts, levis, and windbreakers. The struggle was over what to actually do with my life, rather than over what I believed. What I believed was never in question. But being a pastor was somewhere near the bottom of my list. Oh, I respected Dad—so much so that I knew I could never be like him. And people who knew both of us agreed. I was so "unpreacherlike"—whatever that is.

But by my eighteenth birthday, I was not only convinced that God was calling me, I had become convinced that I could do nothing else. I had reached that conclusion after prayer, internal debate, and numerous circumstantial signs. Still, my attitude toward being a pastor remained ambivalent. Even when I enrolled in college, I was not quick to admit to folks that I was studying for the ministry.

Late one Friday night, in the meat market where I was working as a part-time butcher, a customer pried into my true intentions. I had cleaned the floor, the butcher block, and most of the knives. The one last browsing customer who had gotten in as the door was being locked stood scratching her head in front of the meat case. I waited impatiently for her to make up her mind so I could close up and go home to study. She was a happy, gregarious, large black lady.

"You're new around here, ain't you?" she said as she examined me.

"Yes, I am."

"You go to the college?" she pressed.

"Yes, I do."

"Whatcha studying?" she asked.

"Well..." I was not prepared for her examination, and my answer must have sounded tentative: "Well, I'm studying to be a preacher."

She laughed loudly. "Boy, you don't study to be no preacher; either you is or you ain't!"

No one had ever explained it to me quite that way. As I thought it over afterwards, she was right. I *was* a preacher. I needed to admit it. Sure I needed to study, but study would not settle the issue. Seeing it this way, I was willing to be identified as a preacher because, like it or not, that is what I was.

In the summer of 1957, at the age of twenty, I was asked to serve a small Baptist church in Mobile, Alabama, as interim, then permanent, pastor. I was ordained December 1, 1957.

In addition to pastoral duties, for two years I commuted the one hundred miles from Mobile, Alabama, to William Carey College in Hattiesburg, Mississippi. During those two years education and pastoring competed for my attention, and to some extent they both suffered. I began to see both pastoring and education in a different light. My idealism soon gave way to reality.

My first funeral as a pastor was for a church member's relative who had committed suicide. Dad's pastoral advice to me was, "Your job is not to determine the destination of the deceased, but to comfort those who remain with the word and presence of God." But the pastor who assisted me felt obliged to inform the family and friends about the probability that the deceased did not make heaven.

Before long, I faced the deaths of a five-year-old who had Hodgkin's disease, a seventeen-year-old with Hodgkin's disease, and a twelve-year-old with a brain tumor—all beautiful girls. Then there was another suicide. There were other funerals for aged Christians who had lived full lives, and there were weddings, births, and baptisms. By the time I had graduated from college in 1959, I had also graduated from a lot of naiveté. I had learned that words—academic or religious—can be empty. Only presence seemed to help—the presence of love, sincerity, understanding, and, most of all, the presence of God.

Somewhere in between visiting church members, prospective members, the sick, and the bereaved, and presiding over funerals, weddings, and church meetings, I found an answer to my prayers for a wife. Carolyn's father was a local physician, and we were introduced in 1958 through a mutual friend. Next to choosing to serve the Lord, choosing her was the best and most important choice I ever made. From 1960 to 1963, she and I attended New Orleans Baptist Theological Seminary.

One could debate the effects of studying and pastoring at the same time. Added to the stress of competing demands was a critical attitude on my part. I was theologically a fundamentalist, pastoring a growing church. My youth, zeal, biblical views, and practical experience with certain realities may have made me uneducable. I had little time for any professor who expressed doubt about the Bible's authenticity or inspiration. I also had little time for professors who lacked a relationship with the real world of practical reality. Several professors seemed to me to fall into one of those categories. Commuting twice a week from Mobile to New Orleans and other driving added up to one thousand miles per week and many hours. On one front I faced Greek, Hebrew, and theology; on the other I faced sermons, visitations, weddings, and funerals. On one front I faced hypotheses, theories, speculation and doubt; on the other I faced cold reality and the demand for faith. My heart caved in. In November of 1962 I experienced all of the symptoms of a heart attack. I was taken to the hospital and examined. The attending physician told me that I was under severe stress and advised me to quit something. In early 1963, I quit seminary.

TWO

Something More

BY THE SPRING OF 1963 THE CHURCH, Bay View Heights Baptist Church, was regularly hitting a Sunday attendance of three hundred, and we had good growth statistics to report to our local association of the Southern Baptist Convention. I was attending denominational functions, serving as secretary of the pastor's conference, and playing golf with some of my new pastor friends. Carolyn and I were expecting our first child. We lived in a nice home in the growing part of the city. I was also a member of the Lion's Club and did charity work.

On the surface it would seem that the game plan for becoming a successful pastor was working. I was not out of school long, however, before I realized that I was not really prepared to do the job.

Perhaps it was the golf partner who died as I stood by his hospital bed praying for him. Maybe it was my constant battle with tobacco, which I wanted to give up but couldn't. Maybe it was the demand of three sermons each week, or my lack of spiritual depth, or numerous tests and temptations that made me know I could not go on pastoring as I understood it. Whatever the factors, I was only twenty-six years old and already at a spiritual dead end.

Our church was adding to its building facilities. The contractor, Darrell Booker, was a man for whom I had worked in my teens. Each week he would come by and talk with me about the Lord and the building process—in that order.

Mr. Booker was in his mid-sixties; he stood tall and had a full head of grey hair. Sometimes when he talked about the Lord his eyes would fill with tears and he would lift his hand up toward the Lord. I thought this unusual, but his devotion seemed very real.

"Mr. Booker, I love the Lord, but I don't seem to love him like you do."

"Charles, I know what you want to hear about. Did I ever tell you about the time I was baptized in the Holy Spirit?"

"No, sir."

"You know, I have been a Baptist deacon for many years and have built several churches here in Mobile. But I am going to tell you something I don't tell everybody because they wouldn't understand. When I was a young man, they had camp meetings out in the country that would go on for weeks. One night, I went out with the evangelist to pray before the meeting began. I knelt down by an old stump and began to pray. Before long I felt the presence of God in a powerful way, and the Holy Spirit seemed to come down upon me, and I began to praise God in a heavenly language."

His eyes filled with tears and his face seemed to glow as he relived the experience.

"Charles, did you ever hear of Charles G. Finney?"

"Yes, sir. Dad has referred to him many times over the years."

"Ever read his biography?" he asked.

"No, sir."

"I'm going to bring it to you. It tells how he was filled with the Spirit."

Soon Mr. Booker brought the book. Academic and pastoral hunger had left me so dry that I devoured it.

Finney had been an attorney and an agnostic. He told of a day-long session out in the woods seeking God. Late that evening, after having found peace with God, he continued seeking God back in his office. He said that as he turned to put a log on the fire, he received a mighty baptism with the Holy Spirit and fire. The Spirit of God came upon him like "waves of liquid love." He went on to say that he fairly "bellowed the unutterable gushings of his soul."

The testimonies of Darrell Booker and Charles G. Finney impressed me deeply. I was to hear another one.

Ken Sumrall was a pastor friend in Pensacola, Florida. We had met in seminary and became good friends, exchanging pulpits and times of fellowship. Now he was preaching a series of meetings at a Baptist church in Mobile County and testifying to being baptized in the Holy Spirit.

On a Monday night I drove out to the small Baptist church where he was preaching the series of meetings. He was standing at the front door as I drove up. I got out and walked toward him, feeling cautious because of the things that I had heard.

"Charles!" he grabbed me and hugged me. It was unexpected, and I knew something had happened. His preaching was different. And a baby with a defective heart was healed that week at the services. There was ample evidence that something was going on—something different. Ken gave me a copy of a tape that had his testimony on it. I took it home and played it. Again my heart was stirred.

The following week I drove the sixty miles to Pensacola, Florida, where Ken and those with him were having prayer meetings. As soon as I walked in the renovated store building where they were gathering, I felt the presence of God. About thirty people were praying, singing, reading Scripture, sharing thoughts, and waiting on the moving of the Holy Spirit. I sat in the back. Before I realized it, nearly five hours had passed. I was amazed.

The following week I was back. This time I sat closer. I searched the Scriptures as I prayed and tried to listen for any word from the Lord. I had a growing sense of God's blessing and an expectation of his fullness. I opened my Bible in the dimly lit room to read Romans 14:17, "The kingdom of God is not food and drink, but righteousness and peace and joy in the Holy Spirit."

I read it again. I chuckled deep within as I read "joy in the Holy Spirit."

"He's going to get it laughing!"

I turned and saw two ladies behind me praying. Embarrassed, but happy, I began to look for a private place. There wasn't one. In the back corner was a small partition the size of a blackboard. I went behind it to pray in the corner. But the board wasn't as tall as I, nor did it go all the way to the floor, so I bent over. I had planned to beg God to fill me with the Holy Spirit but found that I could only praise him. Soon I was upright, hands lifted, gushing out in praise the love and joy I had found in Jesus Christ.

The sixty-mile drive back to Mobile was unlike any trip I had ever made. I was intoxicated, but sober; joyful, but serious; fulfilled, but curious about the future. I knew this would have professional implications. Ken had been asked to leave his church. Possibly I would, too.

In seven years Bay View Heights Baptist Church had grown from thirty to three hundred in attendance. The people were good to Carolyn and me. Many good things had happened. But though attendance was good, we hadn't had any recent conversions. I was dry; so was our baptistry. No one would respond to the invitation to come forward and commit their lives to Christ. But the following Sunday was different. My text was Matthew 3:11: "I baptize you with water for repentance, but he who is coming after me is mightier than I, whose sandals I am not worthy to carry; he will baptize you with the Holy Ghost and with fire." My title was "Something Extra!" John the Baptist baptized in water, but Jesus had a mightier baptism than that of water—the Holy Spirit and fire. Before I could finish my sermon, people began coming forward. Many were weeping and praying to be filled with the Spirit. I was more amazed than anyone. I just stopped preaching, waited awhile, and dismissed the meeting.

One member walked up to me afterward and said, "I don't know where you've been, but I want to go there."

THREE

... and Fire

THANK GOD FOR DAD. Each Sunday after the morning service, Carolyn and I would drive the seven miles to Dad's and Mom's home for Sunday dinner. This Sunday would be different. I was still brimming with the joy and excitement of the Spirit.

As usual Dad called on me to ask the blessing on the food. I don't remember what I said or how long I prayed; but when I finished, the table talk was subdued. After lunch Dad said, "Charles, could we go back into my room and talk?"

"Yes, sir." Somehow it sounded like the times when I was growing up and was about to receive correction. "He's heard about my experience," I thought; so I loaded up my guns with Acts 2 and 1 Corinthians 12.

He was serious. "Charles, I listened to your prayer and sense that you are closer to God perhaps than I've ever known you to be."

"Thank you, sir."

"Charles, have you been speaking with tongues?" I couldn't imagine how he knew. "Yes, Dad, I have, but..."

"No, Charles, that is between you and the Lord. But may I give you some advice?" His small blue eyes pierced me. His grey hair and sober demeanor drew forth the respect I had always had for him.

"Yes, sir."

"Charles, something has happened to you, and you've gotten into the spiritual realm. But you have only been there a few days. Satan, your enemy, has been there since before time began. Don't get to thinking that you know a whole lot—you hear?"

"Yes, sir," I heard. I wanted to crawl under the bed.

For six months the enemy didn't show up in any obvious way. Our church broke all records for attendance, baptisms, and finances, right through the summer of 1964. People were meeting for prayer and being blessed. All seemed orderly and prosperous.

It was in the fall that things began to unravel. The deacons and I were meeting in my office. One of the deacons, who had served longer than the others, reached out and took a small green book off my book shelf. The book was entitled *What Baptists Believe and Why They Believe It*. I always gave each new member a copy of that book.

The deacon asked me a question that I had dreaded for months.

"Brother Charles, do you speak in tongues?"

I paused. The church's future and mine rested on that question.

"Yes, I do in my private devotions." I answered truthfully.

He gently shook the little green book in my direction.

"Brother Charles, speaking in tongues is not in here."

I reached over on to my desk and picked up a much larger black book and shook it in his direction.

"No, sir, but it is in here. And this is the book that I was called to preach."

The lines were drawn. Contrary to my deepest hopes, the church began choosing sides. Needless to say, the spirit of revival stopped as the people became embroiled in controversy—a controversy which quickly spread outside our church to the denominational apparatus.

In the next few months I lost over twenty-five pounds and the church lost one hundred members. Now I know what John the Baptist meant when he said, "... and fire!"

For months I studied the Scriptures. For weeks at a time, I and a few friends would wait before the Lord at night in prayer—sometimes, all night. For the first time I had to thoroughly examine my call: What was I called to preach? to build? What is the church? How should it be governed? Is it a democracy? What is a body? How do the gifts of the Spirit operate?

It was a miracle that I was not fired. My resignation was put to a vote, but only eleven people voted for me to resign, while one hundred fifty-nine voted for me to stay. Many would not vote, but left nevertheless.

Some deacons resigned and left the church. This caused me great pain, and it caused them great pain as well. The fear that our church would become wild and heretical stampeded others.

The other deacons chose to stay in the church, but they resigned as deacons because they too were reexamining what deaconship was from a biblical standpoint. Virtually every major church officer resigned. When the members voted, I told them that if I stayed my first effort would be to teach the book of Acts with a view to being a New Testament church. I further warned them that I would advocate the gifts of the Spirit and would preach wherever and whatever the Lord led. They voted for me on those conditions. Now I was free to examine the Scriptures and obey God in a way that I had never been before.

"After the fire," we were left with one hundred and fifty people who wanted to know the Lord better and realized that there was more to know than we had ever imagined. We were all driven to our knees and to our Bibles. In the ensuing months several convictions emerged that changed my course and the course of those who would be following:

1. The church depends on prayer and the power of the Holy Spirit. The church is essentially a spiritual organism.

2. The church is a body. A body has headship and joints that connect, communicate, and coordinate so that it can move toward meaningful purposes.
3. The church is not a democracy. While every believer is a priest, God sets leaders and gifts in the body to lead it into his purpose. God's purpose is not always supported by the majority.
4. The church was never intended to operate without the gifts of the Holy Spirit. If the church is the body of Christ, then the power of the Holy Spirit has to work through it as it did through Christ in his incarnation.

While the battle for spiritual gifts had been won in our local congregation, we were still part of the larger Baptist community, and we wanted to remain there. Our local struggle had not gone unnoticed. Members who left us went to other Baptist churches and told their grievance: "They are not really Baptist."

We wanted to be. I owed Baptists so much. I was born in a Baptist hospital, a Baptist pastor's son. I grew up in Baptist churches, was educated in Baptist schools, and married a wonderful Baptist girl in First Baptist Church. For seven years I had pastored a Baptist church.

We were still Baptist in many ways. Theologically, I held to my Baptist training. We continued to function in the denominational structure. However, we were also different in some ways. We worshiped more demonstratively, we made room for people to share their gifts in the services in orderly ways, and we prayed for the sick with the conviction that the church ought to be in the healing ministry.

There were other differences of an ecclesiastical nature. In previous years the deacons had been a board of directors that acted as representatives of the church congregation to balance pastoral authority. We had never had any serious difficulties with that—though we had never had a serious contest of wills. But when I was baptized in the Spirit, the relationship changed. The deacons challenged me and my spiritual experience. The deacons were pressured to get me voted out of the church because of my spiritual experience and because of their own sense of duty to the denomination and Baptist tradition. But when I insisted on bringing the issue to the entire church body for a vote, the deacons lost by a large margin. In a sense, the Baptist political concept lost the vote of the church as well. All of the deacons resigned.

For a time after that I was the only church leader. As I and fellow servants of Christ prayed and studied, we became convinced of the need for a plurality of church leaders who shared responsibility. Soon we appointed elders, who in fact bore spiritual responsibilities for caring for designated parts of the flock. These men were open to the charismatic dimension. They were not so much a board of directors as fellow shepherds. We soon formed a leadership of men who earned a share of authority because they shared pastoral responsibility. Eventually, each elder had responsibility for one of the small groups that met in homes.

I saw the need to train these men in the Bible, spiritual gifts, ministry functions, and caring for the other members of the church. It was a most fulfilling pastoral experience. But it made us governmentally different from other Baptist churches in our area. We were charismatic and were now governed by a presbytery of elders who had been appointed by the pastor.

The church had internal peace and growth, and I began to get invitations to speak to other groups and churches. Much of my time was spent traveling and ministering to a wide variety of groups.

In late 1969, I became involved with *New Wine* magazine in Fort Lauderdale, Florida, and in 1970 became a committed member of a fellowship of nondenominational teachers, which included Derek Prince, Bob Mumford, and Don Basham. Later, Ern Baxter also became a part of our fellowship.

Derek was then about fifty-five years old, a graduate of

Cambridge University in England, and a King's Scholar. Bob was about forty, a graduate of Reformed Episcopal Seminary in Philadelphia. Don, about forty-two, was a graduate of Phillips University in Enid, Oklahoma. None of us shared much in the way of theological or cultural background. What we did share was a moment in history when God was pouring out his Spirit and calling us to teach and train as many people as we could to respond to his lordship.

It seemed clear that God was pushing me out of my Baptist pulpit and drawing me into an emerging movement, as yet undefined but full of promise. In 1971, with mixed emotions, I resigned from Bay View Heights Baptist Church of Mobile, Alabama, and recommended a new charismatic Baptist pastor. In addition, I recommended the church's continued relationship to our Baptist denomination.

For fourteen years I had pastored that church. It was my entire ministry. The last seven years had been a new beginning in the Holy Spirit and a constant walk through the fire of testing. The fire had burned away much of my life that was bad, and much that was good also. In the course of these years, Carolyn had been filled with the Holy Spirit, and we had two dear children. As we packed to move to Fort Lauderale, she told me that there would soon be a third.

FOUR

Pastoring People

UNTIL 1971 I HAD THOUGHT of myself as the pastor of a Baptist church. Now I was the pastor of a Baptist church no longer. But once again I was to find out that I was a pastor; not because I had a local church, but because that is what I was.

The rental truck was loaded, towing an extra trailer. Carolyn followed in one car, and Jeanie, my secretary, followed in another. Our entourage moved through Tallahassee, Florida, where we stopped for the night. I called Gerrit Gustafson, who had interned at Bay View Heights and was living in Tallahassee. We had sent him from Mobile to Tallahassee where he had a house ministry to youth and street people.

"Gerrit, I am on my way to Fort Lauderdale. We are going by faith; I believe that's where God wants us. Perhaps the Lord will lead you to join us there. Something is happening there that is drawing some leaders together."

Gerrit responded that he would pray about it and perhaps join us later. The next morning we got up early to leave. Gerrit was at the truck. He said that the Lord had spoken to him not to delay or look back, and he was ready to go immediately. Now there were six of us on the journey—myself, Carolyn, two children, Jeanie, and Gerrit. It dawned on me that I was still a pastor, not of a church but of five other people—each one an individual with special needs and gifts.

We had not finished unpacking in Fort Lauderdale before a

minister dropped by and said that perhaps I should take over his pulpit. I declined his gracious offer. I was spending too much time in travel and board meetings associated with *New Wine* magazine and its related ministries. Nevertheless, I had people to care for. Gerrit and Jeanie lived in our home for a time. Other couples began to come over—Mike and Pat Reed, John and Cherie Norwood, Ed and Carole Raite, and Tommy and Diane Richters. Soon I was the pastor of a small flock that met in our home from time to time.

I pastored people. I found myself loving them and caring about what happened in their lives. We really did not consider ourselves a church. All of us attended other churches. My family would have joined a local Baptist church, but after I shared my experience with the pastor, he requested that we just attend but not join.

In the spring of 1972, two men came to Fort Lauderdale from Colorado to a conference we sponsored. They requested that I visit their town and help establish a church. I could not go because of previous commitments, but I recommended that Gerrit go. They received that recommendation, and he went.

His first letter back to me made a sobering request. "Brother Charles, you are my spiritual father. You sent me. I don't want to feel like I am alone. When Jesus sent his disciples he said, 'Lo, I am with you.' Will you be with me? Paul continued to care for Timothy and Titus. Will you continue to be my pastor? I need your support."

My thoughts turned to other men and women who had looked to me for leadership and support, and now had been sent to other cities and nations. There was Hugo Zelaya, a Costa Rican who had lived in Mobile and had served as an elder in our local church. He had returned to Costa Rica as a Bible teacher and pastor. He was there partly because of my leadership.

Then there was Terry Parker, who had left the service station business and was ministering full time. He, too, was struggling to reach his pastoral potential in Christ.

Glen Roachelle was in Pascagoula, Mississippi, pastoring a small flock. He was a Pentecostal whose district superintendent asked him to leave his denomination for associating with me. "What a switch," I thought. I knew lots of Baptists who were asked to leave for fellowshipping with Pentecostals, but this Pentecostal was put out for fellowshipping with a Baptist.

John and Ellen Duke were in New Zealand. John had been my associate in Mobile until I recommended him to a church in New Zealand. They were a long way from home. What responsibility did I have to them?

Gerrit's letter had raised a great question. Until then, I had thought only of local churches and responsibilities. As a Baptist, I was skeptical about authority and responsibility that extended beyond the local church body. But one by one, these people were reminding me that I pastored people—not a church structure.

Finally, I wrote Gerrit. "Yes, I will accept responsibility. Let me know what I can do to help you. I will lift you to the Lord in my prayers." Somehow I sensed that I had said yes to more than I understood.

Again I was drawn back to the word of God. I recalled a night years earlier when Ken Sumrall, two other men, and I spent the night in prayer in Pensacola. There were no fireworks that night. But about 3:00 A.M. the Lord spoke to me out of Colossians about Jesus: "*He* is the image of the invisible God. In *him* all the fullness of God dwells. *Christ* in you is the hope of glory. In *whom* are hid all the treasures of wisdom and knowledge. Rooted and built up in *him*. In *him* dwells all the fullness of the Godhead bodily."

That night it had not seemed so profound at first. True, it was all in Jesus; I knew that. But as I had driven home from the prayer meeting with the sun coming up, I knew God had blocked out all other revelation that night so that I would remember the main point: Jesus Christ is the incarnation of all truth and wisdom. He is the divine pattern in all things.

Now, free of the regular responsibilities of a church pastor, but nonetheless relating as a pastor to people, I looked afresh at the pattern of Jesus, the Pastor. I looked at how he related to those individuals whom he pastored, to find a model for how I should relate to the individuals that I pastored. My view of pastoring was undergoing fundamental change from institutional to personal relationships. This had radical implications. I didn't intend to be radical, but the idea was.

As I studied the gospels, it became quite clear that Jesus was contending with an impersonal view of pastoral care. The problem in Israel was not a lack of religious leaders. There was an abundance of religious leaders. The temple and synagogues flourished. Yet Israel was in a terrible condition: sickness and demonization, doubt and cynicism, a carnal view of the kingdom of God. Religious leaders were blind, legalistic, and unmerciful; they loved power and prestige; they proselytized but disdained personal care. Israel had many rabbis, but few shepherds. They seemed better suited to Roman rule than to the government of God.

The failure of the Jewish ecclesiastical system had become a dark backdrop for Jesus Christ, the good Shepherd. Judaism's fundamental weakness in the days of Christ was that it did not spiritually and materially care for the people of God. In contrast, the fundamental strength which Jesus revealed was the love of God for his people, his power to help them, and his ability to care for their whole lives. The Jewish system was not evil; it was God-ordained. But any system without the Spirit becomes uncaring.

David, Isaiah, Jeremiah, and Ezekiel had all spoken of a Shepherd who was to come, the Shepherd Messiah who would save God's people. He was to be the good Shepherd who would deliver them from their sins, diseases, and captivities. He would be their governor from God, anointed to bring in the kingdom. He would care for them.

As I looked at chapters like Matthew 23, in which Jesus denounces the Jewish ecclesiastical failure, I saw the sword of the Spirit—the word of God—cut through the issue. The real issue was personal care for the people of God, rather than an impersonal system of religion. My desire became to pastor God's people the way Jesus did.

Withdrawing from structural pastoral responsibilities had helped me to clarify my role as a pastor. I never viewed my structure as wrong. Nevertheless, it was the withdrawal from the institutional aspects of pastoral care that made me more conscious of the personal needs of people. In a new way I was discovering that I was a pastor—though for the first time in fourteen years, I was not a pastor of a local church. I was, however, a pastor to Gerrit, John, Terry, Glen, Hugo—and who else?

FIVE

Extending the Chief Shepherd's Care

MY EXPERIENCE HAD LED ME to the conviction that pastoring was a personal relationship that existed beyond institutional responsibilities. In fourteen years of pastoral ministry, I had often experienced conflict between the two roles. My initial call to pastoral ministry seemed intensely spiritual and involved with people. But the more I succeeded the more I became something else—a manager.

Toward the end of my pastorate in 1971 I had nightmares over what might be happening to unattended members—the new Christians and the peripheral members. I recalled the man and woman who divorced their mates and married each other, all while attending our church almost every Sunday. I knew nothing of the episode until weeks afterward. Other grievous situations went unnoticed while the leaders concentrated on maintaining their administrative and educational duties, and giving care to the core of the church—those who needed it least.

As experience drove me back to the Bible, the Bible reinforced my conviction that pastoring was personal. The biblical references to shepherds repeatedly drove the point home. Psalm 23 represents the clearest picture of personal pastoral care by describing the care of a shepherding Lord.

John 10 also describes the Lord as a personal shepherd. Matthew 18:12 tells about a shepherd who leaves the ninety-nine and goes after one that had strayed.

Numerous times in the Old Testament the Messiah is referred to as a shepherd. The Hebrew word *râ'âh* is used to describe our Lord's mission in Isaiah 40:11, Psalm 80:1, Psalm 23:1, Ezekiel 34:12, 23, and Ezekiel 37:34. The term *râ'âh*, which means to feed or lead as a shepherd, is used over forty times in the Old Testament. It is also used to describe other ministries besides that of the Messiah himself.

In 1 Peter 5:4, Jesus is not only called the Shepherd, he is called the Chief Shepherd. He is the Shepherd who begets all other shepherds and is the example for their ministry. The Greek word *pŏimainō* which means to feed, tend or rule as a shepherd, and the word *pŏimēn* which means shepherd, are used eight times in the New Testament referring to spiritual leaders other than Jesus Christ. Jesus is the Chief Shepherd, but not the only shepherd. His desire is to raise up other shepherds who are delegated to extend his concerns to his people.

A most telling verse in my changing view of personal pastoral care was Ephesians 4:11: "And his gifts were that some should be apostles, some prophets, some evangelists, some pastors and teachers..." The word translated "pastors" translates the Greek for "shepherds." The ascended Christ would not merely send institutional leaders who could carry out professional duties; he would send shepherds—like himself.

I also discovered in the Scriptures that God had a fondness for shepherd leaders. Abraham, Moses, and David were all shepherds before becoming leaders among the people of God. It seemed that shepherding a flock of sheep helped prepare them. God seemed to elevate very few priests into national prominence—but often chose shepherds.

Of course, shepherd is not the only word which describes Christ's relationship to his people. He is called the captain of an army, the head of a body, the vine which supports branches, the king of the nation, and the bridegroom of a bride. All of those descriptions deserve attention. But none is used more often nor more effectively than the word shepherd. Jay Adams, a noted author on the subject of pastoral counseling, defines a shepherd as "the one who provides full and complete care for the flock." Based on my studies of the pastoral calling, I came to view the shepherd or pastor as the "extension of Christ's own love and care for his people."

Whether one uses the title "shepherd" when referring to a pastor is not the issue. It is a matter of substance, not title. Under the old covenant, the time came when true prophets could not identify with those who were called prophets, and when those who were called shepherd, were not indeed shepherds (see Amos 7:14-15). When men bear any spiritual titles and do not function spiritually, they bring judgment on themselves.

While Psalm 23 describes how Christ himself functions as a shepherd, it also describes how those who extend Christ's love for his people ought to care for them. "My shepherd" indicates a personal relationship and responsibility. The relationship results in:

—Provision for all needs
—Rest in pleasant places
—Quiet direction
—Restoration for the weary soul
—A protective presence in the dark valleys
—Comfort with correction and direction
—Nourishment in the midst of enemies
—Overflow of personal blessings
—Life filled with goodness and love
—Dwelling in God's house

While no mere human pastor can assure all of these benefits, a human pastor can be an instrument of the Chief Shepherd and the extension of his concern. Any shepherd who shows a lack of interest in these areas raises questions about his relationship to the Chief Shepherd.

It is interesting to note that the apostolic teaching expressed in Acts 20:17 and following extends the same quality of care described in Psalm 23.

When Jesus describes his own ministry in John 10, he calls himself the good shepherd. He affirms his messianic fulfillment of Old Testament prophecies that God would provide a shepherd. In verse three he says that he knows his sheep by name, affirming that true pastoral care is personal.

Certainly Jesus' own shepherding ministry was unique. Peter reminded the undershepherds of his day that only the Chief Shepherd died for the people and they belong to him alone. He purchased them with his own blood. This the undershepherds could not do. They may lay down their lives. But they only extend the care of Christ; they do not possess the flock.

Of course, any metaphor breaks down when pressed too far. Ours is not a shepherding culture, so in some ways the metaphor seems far removed from us. Nevertheless, as I studied the Bible, I became convinced that in the shepherd I had my best definition of how I ought to function as a pastor.

Having reached these conclusions, I believed that the shepherd metaphor provided a biblical basis for reinterpreting my view of pastoral ministry. I saw the pastor not as an official presiding over a religious institution, but as an extension of Christ's care for His people in a personal way.

How would Psalm 23 apply to my relationship with Hugo, Gerrit, John, or the others? For one thing, it meant that I had to keep their personal needs in mind. I could not separate my personal success from their well-being. If I was their shepherd appointed by Jesus the Chief Shepherd, then I was his servant to assist in caring for and leading their lives. I began to pray for them daily. I carried them and others in my heart before the Lord.

When I sat down for dinner, I wondered if Hugo had plenty to eat in Costa Rica. When I prayed, I wondered if John needed encouragement in New Zealand. I wondered if Glen was receiving support in Pascagoula. I had to get involved with them.

It was those concerns that led me to curtail my travel ministry in 1973 and to concentrate on training leaders in pastoral care. It also caused me to move into the Mississippi-Alabama Gulf Coast region and work with small groups, trying to answer my own questions about how the care of Christ should be practically applied in church life.

Glen Roachelle, John Duke, who returned from New Zealand, and Terry Parker joined me in the formation of a body of pastors in August 1973. Each had responsibility for small care groups which joined together to form what became Gulf Coast Covenant Church. I had already trained and pastored these three men in some measure. To these men and others with them, I owe a great debt because they walked with me into a grand and often controversial experiment. We had great moments in the presence of God and great trials in seeing how challenging it is to turn vision into reality. It was out of our fellowship and the fellowship of other leaders that the following pages were written in our hearts.

Part II:
Who Is Qualified

SIX

Call

BY 1973 I HAD BECOME CONVINCED that the pastor was a type of shepherding leader who gave individual care to the flock in addition to providing it overall leadership. If that was true, how could the church produce enough of these kind of leaders?

The church produced leaders with preaching and academic skills, but could it produce enough shepherds? Could it produce more leaders who were comfortable in personal relationships, meeting life's realities with their people?

While the context in which I faced the question in 1973 was new—outside an established church structure—the question had been with me since the time I was baptized in the Spirit. At that time I had received a prophecy from the Lord while in a men's prayer meeting. In my mind, I had seen a farm and a large farm house. I sensed God saying, "When the harvest is not yet ready, don't sit on the porch and wait. Pay attention to your barn, your tools, and your laborers. Get prepared because when the harvest comes in, it will come in all at once. And it will be so large that you won't be able to bring it all in. In fact, you will weep because you cannot bring it all in. You will drop some along the way as you are bringing it back to the barn. It is time now to prepare your laborers and your tools and to increase your ability to conserve the harvest."

That prophetic word did not make much sense to me at the time in 1965, because Bay View Heights had lost over one hundred members and no harvest was in sight. However, I took it to heart. I tried to teach our men how to study the Scriptures, how to care for God's people, and how to move in the Holy Spirit. For the most part, these people were not professionally trained to be ministers. They had little or no understanding of Greek and Hebrew, of exegetical and homiletical principles. But they did have a real concern for God's people, and they were genuine in their faith. It was my responsibility, I realized, to teach them the skills that would enable them to translate their sincerity into productivity.

As I did so, I began to study the process of how new leaders emerge in the church. I looked into what their qualifications should be and how they should be recognized and sent forth into the service of Christian leadership. I spent many hours in prayer meetings with the core of our church leadership. I watched their responses to the Holy Spirit. I spent many hours in Bible study with them trying to prepare for the harvest. I spent time in their homes. At first, I had felt guilty for being so close to some and not as close to others—but then I saw the same principle in Jesus' life, as he spent time with those who were to become leaders of his church.

One night in 1965 I visited in the home of Terry and Charlotte Parker, a couple that was emerging in leadership, and we prayed together. Their young daughter was in another room, coughing incessantly. I asked if we could pray for her, and they agreed. We went to her bed and prayed as the presence of God hovered over. She was instantly healed. Our faith and awareness of God was high. As we returned to the living room God spoke to me, telling me that this couple would be as Priscilla and Aquila to me. I didn't recall who Priscilla and Aquila were. I looked them up and remembered that they were the apostle Paul's companions. Later, Terry and Charlotte traveled with me in ministry and shared much of my pastoral burden in the local church. Together they led hundreds of people into a deeper life in Christ.

About a year after the prophetic word, Bay View Heights had begun to grow again. New people were added who were not spiritually mature but were hungry for the things of God. One by one the men and women I had trained entered into some kind of Christian leadership.

Now, in 1973, I was beginning a new local church with a new structure. Some of those I had trained and pastored earlier were with me again, training and pastoring others. We were exploring in a new setting the whole issue of how to identify the qualities of leadership in a caring congregation.

Our experience over the years that followed could be crystalized by saying that we learned that pastoral leaders in the church need a call from God, godly character, natural capacities, and spiritual gifting. The church belongs to Jesus Christ. He died for it and purchased it with his own blood. He intercedes for it and is its head. Anyone who claims to have a role in it must be authorized by him. He or she must be called to care by the Lord himself. All ministry in the church is first of all a response to him, a response to his call.

Jeremiah 23 offers a discussion of the difference between true and false prophets. The primary issue in distinguishing true and false prophets is not the authenticity of the message they declare but the authenticity of their calling. What makes a false prophet false is not simply his preaching a false message, but his preaching under false pretenses: he is not truly authorized; he was never sent by God.

A false practitioner of medicine may on occasion offer sound medical advice. But he is a fake in any case because he is not what he is posing to be. He is not authorized by a board of examiners. Each ministry in the church must be called and set in place by him. Scripture makes it clear that he sets the gifts in the body as he wills, that all service in the body is unto him, and that being set in their place by him is the basis for anyone functioning and exercising authority in the church. The call of the Lord is the first step toward authentic ministry (Eph 4:11).

The Bible provides numerous examples of men being called. Exodus 3 and 4 speak of Moses' call. Isaiah 6 tells about Isaiah's call, and Jeremiah 1 about Jeremiah's call.

A sense of divine calling not only sets one's ministry into motion, but it enables one to withstand the difficulties that inevitably come. Many times I have been frustrated because I sought to build leadership around someone who had ability but who was not called to be a pastoral leader. Inevitably, the grace will be lacking for such a person and he or she will break under the load of responsibility. I once experienced God showing me that I was functioning in leadership outside his call. At one point in the early 1970s, in the midst of an impossible schedule, God showed me that some of my ministry was false—not false in content but false in the sense of lacking his authorization. I was going some places where I had not been sent.

On the other hand, the sense of God's calling has at times been especially important for me. In 1966 when I was facing the crisis with my denomination over my Pentecostal practices, God renewed my conviction of his call to me. One morning, when my denomination was to begin its annual meeting in our area, the Lord awakened me around 4:00 A.M. I went into the living room to pray, seek the Lord, and study the Bible. God called my attention to John 15:16: "You did not choose me, but I chose you and appointed you that you should go and bear fruit and that your fruit should abide." It made a powerful impact on me as I realized again that God had called me. My ministry was established on his call. He had not only called me to minister, but he had called me to the particular place I now found myself. There was a certain destiny involved. I was greatly encouraged to know that I would be fruitful and that my fruit would remain in spite of the controversy and various problems I faced.

Happily, I was not removed from the denomination. I was given additional years to fellowship with my Baptist brethren and try to demonstrate the dynamics that had entered my life.

Our experience of God's call is a difficult thing to describe. It is a subjective, spiritual experience rather than an objective, merely rational experience. However, many objective and rational factors may be involved. Usually, there is much soul-searching, and one only gradually comes to the conclusion pastoral leadership is the will of God. A call can be like the operation of a mercury light. It appears very dim and flickering at first. But the longer it is on, the brighter it burns. When God is calling, flickering indicators can grow to glaring lights. Sometimes, however, a call can be dramatic and instantaneous as was the apostle Paul's call. In either case, it must be convincing both to the minister and the people who are served.

A call touches one's sense of personal destiny. When one is truly called by God, he begins to realize that this is why he was formed. It satisfies an inner desire; the person realizes that the only way to be fulfilled is through that ministry.

On one occasion I was praying for a fellow pastor whom I had known for several years. He was college and seminary trained and had pastored a successful denominational church. Later, he became involved with the charismatic renewal and went through several transitions. The transitions had left him somewhat confused and frustrated with his ministry. I felt the Lord wanted to clarify and reconfirm his call. I told him that I believed such a confirmation was forthcoming.

Five months later he sat at his desk writing a summary of his concerns, and especially why he had not seen people added to his church. The Lord broke in, "That's your problem. You are trying to lead people to your church, and that's not what I called you to do. I called you to *lead people to Jesus and teach them his ways.*"

Soon the pastor called me, and he was full of joy and renewed enthusiasm. "I know this sounds simple," he said, "but I've heard from God and I've come out of the cave!" He had been hiding in the cave of frustration as Elijah did, because he had lost his sense of divine authorization. The same "still small voice" that sent Elijah back about the Lord's business had spoken to him. His call was renewed and clarified. His confidence and authority were restored. We rejoiced together.

A call gives one a sense of mission. The call of God becomes one's reason for living and one's goal in life. It is a purpose beyond one's self. It is a cause in which to believe. It is the focal point for marshalling all of one's resources to achieve the purposes of God. People are happiest when living for a cause beyond themselves. There is no greater cause than extending the kingdom of God into people's lives.

It is important to realize there are many callings, not just a calling to the clergy, or even to pastoral leadership. Every Christian is redeemed for the purposes of God. Each person has a call on his or her life. The call is not only to conversion to Christ but to the cause of building the church and bearing witness to the kingdom. It is normal for evangelical churches to examine ministers regarding their call to ministry. However, it might be good to examine every church member in the same manner, asking them to tell how they were converted and what their calling is in Christ Jesus.

Jesus Christ is the Great Shepherd. As Glen, John, Terry, and I began to build a new church in the early 1970's, we were convinced that our task in regard to God's people was a shepherding task. If we were going to succeed at that task we would need to build a church that genuinely and practically cared for people. We would need to produce leaders who could extend Jesus' shepherding love, power, and practical care.

We also saw that Jesus' ability was not self-generated. He was called by the Father and sent to the people of God in the power of God. These realizations drove us to look for a somewhat different quality in a leader than we might have sought before: Was he or she called to care? For a pastoral person, whether full-time clergyman or lay pastor, the challenge is to care.

SEVEN

Character

AS WE BEGAN THE NEW CHURCH IN 1973, the character of those who would lead it had become a key concern. This focus stemmed from a new realization of the kingdom of God that had dawned on me the previous year. One experience in particular changed my thinking about the kingdom and drew my attention to the importance of having Christian leaders who embody kingdom character.

It came about this way. The year 1972 had been extremely taxing for me. I was traveling more than half the time, I preached over six hundred times; Carolyn and I had a new baby, and I had assumed responsibilities with *New Wine* magazine as well as producing Bible teaching on cassettes. I was stretched beyond measure.

In December I met in a hotel with three men who were close friends to seek the Lord for his help and guidance. Glen Roachelle, John Duke, Terry Parker, and I met for three days to pray. At the beginning of our time I listened to a cassette which consisted of readings from the book of Psalms to background music. The words of the psalmist washed my weary soul.

After hearing the tape I knelt by the bed to pray. I did something that I never did: I began to pray the Lord's Prayer. It may sound strange, but I regarded the Lord's Prayer in such awe that I was reticent to use it in my personal devotions. On this occasion, I began to groan deeply under the load of weariness. "Our Father...." I spoke slowly. The words tore me as I spoke them. "... who art in heaven ...hallowed be thy name." I could hardly utter the words, realizing that I was speaking to the holy God of heaven and earth. "Thy Kingdom come...." The dam broke; I could no longer control my emotions. I wept deep sobs. I realized that the cry of the Holy Spirit within me was for the kingdom of God to come into my life in a new way. For the first time, I saw that the kingdom of God was already present here on the earth.

I never said the next words, but like a needle stuck on a record they kept going through my mind: "Thy will be done on earth ...thy will be done on earth." I tried to say it but I couldn't. The Spirit was saying it in me, and I heard it.

The experience restored my heart. Since 1964, I had seen many wonderful and powerful things happen through the Spirit. I saw miracles. But I had also seen charisma without character. I had seen the weaknesses that all movements have because movements are made up of people—people using each other for personal advantage, people in immorality becoming casual toward the supernatural. I had become somewhat cynical. What happened in that hotel lifted my attention to Christ, and his kingdom, and the character produced by his leadership. The kingdom of God became my personal pursuit in a more consuming way.

As an evangelical, conversion and soul winning had been my major focus. When I entered the charismatic renewal, the gifts of the Holy Spirit also became a major focus. Now, kingdom became a major focus as well. My attitude toward creation became more positive and aggressive. "Thy will be done on earth" became a mission statement; "The earth is the Lord's!" a battle cry.

A major implication of the new emphasis, I saw, was that the emerging church and its leaders were intended to be an extension of Christ's victory. We would reign with him. We would succeed in Christ where Adam failed. I began to reject any defeatist mentality, any handwringing or glorifying of Satan's power. The church must enjoy the triumph of Christ's resurrection and live in his power. In order to extend Christ's victory in the world, its leaders must demonstrate it in their own lives. His victory must shape their character.

I began to reject any apparent faith or spirituality which had no practical outworking or demonstration. I preached a series of messages under the title, "Righteousness Is More Than Believing." As an evangelical, such a title seemed almost heretical. But the Scriptures speak of men whose faith led them to act. Noah not only believed the flood was coming, he built an ark. He was not saved by the "ark doctrine"; he was saved by the ark, the ark his faith caused him to build.

As we thought of building a new church on such kingdom principles, it was obvious that it would require leaders whose lives were based on them. Natural diligence and godly character would be major requirements for its leaders.

This was clearly the scriptural approach. The apostle Paul instructs Timothy and Titus to examine the character of potential leaders. Charisma without strong character is a bad foundation for church building. While no leader will fully embody all of the elements mentioned in passages such as Titus 1 and 1 Timothy 3, these elements are the standards inspired by God for recognizing any leader in the church. These are the traits formed in men and women who live according to kingdom principles. These traits reflect God's own nature in his people.

Among the apostolic character standards for leadership are these:

1. A good report among people outside the church (1 Tm 3:2). If people outside the church are going to be reached, then they must respect the church. Secular people may not share our values, but they must believe that we are true to our own confession. Since the leaders of the church epitomize what the church stands for, they must be respected by those outside.

King David was judged by God because his sin caused God's

name to be blasphemed among the heathen. God made it clear that he would not tolerate that kind of behavior. A leader's failure to be concerned about God's reputation outside of the church will often bring an intervention from God himself.

2. A man with one wife (1 Tm 3:2). I understand that to mean that a leader should not be a polygamist or unfaithful to his wife. Of course, that does not rule out the possibility that a leader may be celibate.

3. Temperate in the exercise of emotions and appetites (1 Tm 3:2). An overindulgence in one's emotions or appetites can cause one to live for the gratification of the flesh and fall into sin (not to mention bad health). It also renders one insensitive to the Holy Spirit. Proper self-discipline can be observed in physical appearance, health, finances, emotional control, and time management.

4. Prudent (1 Tm 3:2). A leader must possess spiritual wisdom and common sense. Solomon was approved by God for seeking wisdom with which to rule. The book of Proverbs clearly states the desirability of wisdom. The criteria for choosing deacons in the New Testament were that they should be men full of the Holy Spirit and wisdom.

5. Admirable (1 Tm 3:2). The leader should epitomize the best qualities of behavior and evoke esteem both in and out of the church. Admirable leaders can be used by the Spirit to spur youth to aspire to Christian leadership and they can draw the new Christian into church life.

6. Hospitable (1 Tm 3:2). A leader ought to be gracious and open to receiving fellow Christians and strangers alike. A Christian leader's home will often be a place of ministry to those in some kind of need.

7. Able to teach (1 Tm 3:2). The leader should not only be able to express truth verbally but also have the ability to train others to live the Christian life. Some who are skilled verbally are not strong in impartation and training. Others who are not as verbally skilled are nevertheless good at teaching others in practical ways.

8. Not be addicted to alcohol or other drugs (1 Tm 3:3). Addiction is an appetite out of control and a dependency on something other than the Holy Spirit. Substance abuse is a major problem in our society. Any leader who develops such a dependency will lose his place in the kingdom and his ability to represent the lordship of Jesus Christ (1 Cor 6:10). Leaders who fall can be restored, but successful function requires freedom from addictions.

9. Gentle (1 Tm 3:3). This trait recalls the shepherd model. A shepherd is firm but gentle in the application of strength. The Scripture clearly states that gentleness in correction makes it easier for the one corrected to repent. A gentle answer turns away the wrath of the unrepentant.

10. Not a brawler (1 Tm 3:3). A leader is one who has himself physically under control. He is not dependent on his own physical strength but on the Holy Spirit.

11. Not greedy (1 Tm 3:3; 1 Pt 5:2). Greediness is a sure sign of self-centeredness. Generosity indicates that one is truly dependent on the Lord for supply. Generosity also enables God to fulfill many promises made in the Scripture toward the generous (see Is 58; 1 Cor 9; 2 Cor 8 and 9). Tithing is a bare necessity for any leader. One who understands sowing and reaping will go beyond tithing to generosity.

12. One who manages his household well (1 Tm 3:4). One's own house is the first reflection of one's ability to manage. A leader who cannot manage his own household will not be able to manage the house of God. The ability to be a channel of righteousness, peace, and joy into one's own family is the first indicator that an individual has the potential to accomplish that in the church as well. In choosing new leaders, the condition of the leader's family is a major consideration that will indicate what can be expected.

13. One who controls his children with dignity (1 Tm 3:4-5). Parents who manage their children with dignity do not lose control themselves while trying to control their children. A leader who is able to do this will be able to lead the church in trying times, while maintaining the dignity of the pastoral office.

14. Mature and not a novice (1 Tm 3:6). It is impossible to define the precise age for maturity. In the Old Testament, priests were ordained to their office at the age of thirty. The Scriptures indicate that one should be emotionally and spiritually mature before beginning to lead the church. Immaturity will cause one to be vulnerable to pride. One definition of the mature person is one who produces more than he or she consumes. A mature person is a contributor to the well-being of a social unit. An immature person consumes more than he or she produces and needs special attention.

15. Humble (1 Tm 3:6). Humility is lowliness of mind and freedom from pride. Humility indicates that one has come to grips with his or her own sin and has found favor with God. It also indicates that the person is genuinely interested in other people and will be able to listen to them without his own emotions and interests blocking his ability to hear.

Humility is a primary basis for God's promotion. Scripture teaches that humility comes before honor. Therefore, any leader that is going to be honored by God will have to develop humility.

16. Not self-willed or prone to unilateral action, but comfortable with co-operation (Lk 10:1; Acts 15; Gal 2). Nothing tests humility like the ability to act in accord with other people. A self-willed leader will regularly act without prior counsel or approval and will reap the results of his unilateral action. He will also likely produce a constituency that he cannot lead because they have become accustomed to acting unilaterally. Independent, inconsiderate action will scatter the flock.

17. One who enjoys what is good. The true leader finds pleasure in virtuous things. He will not delight in what is immoral, evil or injurious. A person who seems to take delight in other people's pain or embarrassment is not compassionate and does not have good shepherding qualities. I often refer people to Philippians 4:1-9 as good instruction for how to think. A good leader must have learned to think purely and positively.

18. Fair and just (Jas 2:1-13). One of the primary responsibilities of a pastoral leader is to be an instrument of righteousness to the body of Christ through his leadership and the preaching of the gospel. The church is to be an expression of the righteousness and justice of Jesus Christ who shows no partiality. If a leader is not fair-minded and just in dealing with people, he will be unable to bring that characteristic to the church. Churches that show partiality will lose their ability to reach people that Christ died for.

19. Dedicated (Lk 9:57-62). He must not only know what the will of God is but also have the ability to make a commitment and stick to it. His example of dedication and commitment will enable him to marshall his constituents' resources for the accomplishment of God's purpose. He must be single-minded about doing the will of God. Many people with great abilities never realize their full potential because they are not able to dedicate those abilities to a single purpose. A strong commitment to the church's corporate purpose is a primary consideration for potential leaders. Unstable or uncommitted leaders cause major problems.

20. A pastoral leader should be faithful with responsibilities. An erratic response to delegated responsibilities disqualifies a person in the kingdom of God. Luke 16:10-12 clearly teaches this. Jesus said, "He who is faithful in a very little is faithful also in much." It is clear that God will not promote anyone who consistently fails to do little things with diligence. In Luke 16, Jesus extends the faithfulness principle to the use of money and to serving others. A potential pastoral leader should demonstrate the ability to accept assignments and complete them as a matter of personal principle.

Godly character is a substantive issue. It is not merely academic or theoretical; it is not merely an ideal. The qualities of godly character are the behavioral realities of a person's life.

While one may eloquently verbalize the teachings of the faith, character eventually will have a much louder voice and a much more lasting impact.

Inasmuch as the church is the Lord's, we need to bear in mind that he has the right to set the standards for leadership. The church does not set the standards; it obeys them. Both the standard for leadership and the leaders themselves belong to Christ. Pastors are responsible to lay hands on those who meet the approval of the head of the church and the standards of the apostles. To do less is to send unprepared and unauthorized messengers into certain trouble.

The church will reproduce the standards of quality it upholds in its leaders. The church that rejects godly standards in choosing men and women for leadership is abandoning godly standards for its membership. It is a painful thing to see an able leader lose his place because of serious character flaws. It is even more painful to see those same flaws permeate the whole community under his influence. The apostle Paul says in 1 Timothy 5:20 that leaders who continue in sin should be rebuked before their entire constituency. The result should cause all leaders to be aware of the condition of their service and influence.

The years have brought me to a certain realism in regard to the character of leaders in the church. I have realized that

— There are no perfect leaders.

— Communities will tend to get the quality of leadership they deserve and support.

— When leaders fall or fail we cannot undo the damage by "laying off hands."

— Failure is not the occasion to deny our responsibility to leaders and one another. It is the occasion that tests our understanding of the covenant of Jesus' blood.

EIGHT

Capacities

LEADERS HAVE TO HAVE A NATURAL CAPACITY for certain things. Capacity literally means the space to hold. A ship, for instance, might have a capacity of one hundred thousand tons of cargo. Unlike ships, which have a passive capacity, leaders have to grow in their capacities. In fact, a key capacity for a leader is the ability to enlarge his or her capacities to meet the need.

In Matthew 25, Jesus talks about a man who gave amounts of money to his servants. Each servant received an amount commensurate with his capacity to handle it. When the master returned, two of the servants had more. As a result, the master entrusted them with even more. The point is not only that through diligence they had more. The parable also shows that they had become capable of handling more. Their capacities increased. The third servant, however, lost what he had through slothfulness.

Leaders do not seem to be able to be stagnant or keep the status quo. Either they are stretching their capacities, or they are reacting defensively to challenges, losing their resilience and therefore their stewardship. In my early ministry, I failed to see the importance of looking for leaders who could change and broaden their skills.

Through the years I have discovered that some are called to leadership and good character but do not change. But others are adaptable and see the advantage of adjusting their habits, learning new skills, and moving into opportunities. The best investment in potential leadership is the investment that continues to grow.

On one occasion I was on a plane and beside me sat a young man enthusiastic about his work. He was a diver who worked off the reefs in the Caribbean to find exotic aquarium fish. Our conversation turned to sharks. He startled me by saying, "In fact, shark is a popular species for the aquarium."

"Sharks?" I asked. "Don't they get too big?"

"No. They grow to the size of their container. In an aquarium, a shark may only grow to eight or nine inches in its full-grown state. In the ocean, that same fish might reach eight feet."

Just like Christians, I thought. Some Christians stay miniature because they won't deal with the ocean of opportunity. Aquarium Christians are those who prefer the puddle, where they are always able to see the limits of their world. Some leaders are like that. They do not have the capacity to grow with the demands of the Holy Spirit, their flocks, and the mission.

Here are some capacities that a potential leader will need:

1. The capacity to learn. This not only refers to intelligence quotient but also to motivation. The leader must want to serve the purpose of God more effectively.

2. The capacity to communicate. A minister of the gospel needs to sharpen his verbal skills and learn the art of oratory as well as the art of sharing one-to-one. The biblical exemplars of leadership from Noah on were proclaimers. When the audience varies, the leader must adapt to the demands. He puts success over style. Billy Graham said, "When a minister shoots over his congregation's heads, he just proves one thing: he can't shoot."

A pastoral leader should be capable of refuting the gainsayers, those who are cynical regarding the gospel of Jesus Christ. He must have the courage of conviction, the spiritual knowledge, and the verbal skills to be convincing when he talks about the gospel and the great doctrines of the word of God.

3. The capacity to maintain the body-life of the church. A pastor must know the arts of projecting a corporate vision, peacemaking, and utilizing the gifts of his people to achieve the common purpose. Some leaders can go into a nice group and soon it is scattered in several directions. Good leaders know the people and draw them together. The leader must also have the capacity to sense where his people are if he is going to anticipate problems and deal with them before they develop. Some people have great forward vision but poor lateral vision, and they get blind-sided by problems.

4. The capacity for a global perspective. My friend Ern Baxter says, "God is a world person." God's perspective is as broad as creation. His intentions are universal. A pastor with a limited view will not be able to lead his constituents to be an integral part of God's purpose in the whole earth. Prejudice and selfishness severely limit leader's potential.

5. The capacity to handle pressure. There are constant pressures on Christian leaders. There is a spiritual pressure that comes from the adversary; there is internal pressure from one's own demand to do things properly; there is the pressure that comes from among constituents. We can only imagine the kinds of pressures that leaders like Noah, Abraham, Moses, or David were under.

Someone said we must learn to be "laid back" or be "laid out." Any pastor showing signs of coming apart in the midst of pressure will produce scattering and anxiety among his people.

Dad used to say to me, "Remember the sheep watch the shepherd. If the shepherd is afraid, the sheep panic." Composure is an important trait.

6. The capacity for hard work. When I was a boy, I used to walk to school with friends of mine. On more than one occasion we discussed the question of whose daddy had the hardest job. In their eyes, my Dad always seemed to have the easiest job since he was a minister and only had to work one day a week. I could never convince them that pastoring was real work. But anyone who expects to give real care to God's people had better be able to work.

The apostle Paul told the Thessalonians that if anybody would not work, he should not eat. If this is true of the average member of the church, it is certainly true of the leadership. In several biblical passages Paul refers to his labors in the Lord and the hardships he underwent. While all Christian leaders may not face such trials, everyone's work will be tried. The parable of the talents reminds us once again that the Lord despises laziness.

Limited abilities in various areas can be compensated for by the capacities to learn and work. One who is diligent to work and faithful to endure can achieve goals which may never be achieved by a person who has great ability but is weak in diligence and determination.

An unwillingness to develop the natural skills that one has may reveal stubbornness, laziness, or other bad traits. Most of all, it reveals a lack of dedication to God's purposes.

I am greatly indebted in my ministry to Mrs. Loriman, a fifth grade teacher. When I was in high school I became involved in public speaking contests. I was privileged to win several contests and become a state finalist. When I first entered the contests, Mrs. Loriman took an interest in trying to help me, though I had never been a student in her class. She was one of a very few teachers in our rural school that had college training in speech.

Each morning before classes, at her initiative, we would meet in the auditorium. She would stand at one end and I would stand at the other, without a microphone. The auditorium also served as a gymnasium and thus had very poor acoustics. She would make me say my speech across the empty auditorium, pressing me until she could hear every word distinctly. She taught me to project my voice and enunciate my words. She would stop me over and over again in mid-sentence, making me start all over until I could say my speech clearly with some degree of conviction.

One particular word I had a problem with was "farm." I was raised in a small southern community, and the way I said "farm" sounded more like "form." Mrs. Loriman would stop me in the middle of the sentence and shout "farm! farm! farm!" from the other end of the auditorium. I don't know how many times I said farm. But I said it until she was satisfied.

I did not feel the Holy Spirit while this was taking place. Neither did I sense any of God's supernatural power or grace in the whole exercise. I did not feel religious. In fact, many times it made me irate and impatient. I did not consider this a form of spiritual discipline. It was just work. Mrs. Loriman cared enough to make me work. She forced me to encounter my ignorance, stubbornness, laziness, and plain stupidity. She challenged my capacity to learn new and better habits. The degree to which she helped me overcome those things is also the degree to which she prepared me to receive the grace and power of God and to increase the measure of the supernatural in my own life.

Dad used to say to me, "Son, on some subjects you've got enough ignorance to ignorance the whole world." Indeed. Some may think ignorance is bliss, but it is not becoming to a leader in the church. Obvious ignorance distracts from valid gifts. Caring for God's people requires a continual quest for better skills. We must learn to learn.

NINE

Spiritual Gifting

IT MIGHT SEEM OBVIOUS that someone who had seen and experienced the power of the Holy Spirit as I had would rank spiritual gifting high on the list of qualifications for leadership in the church. But as a matter of fact, in the early years of Gulf Coast Covenant Church, I and the other leaders were mildly reacting to problems in the charismatic movement, one of which was that many people who led because of their spiritual gifts were unproven and ill-equipped for leadership. In reaction, I ceased to stress the supernatural element to the degree that I had done when I was first baptized in the Spirit. I continued to regard the supernatural workings of the Spirit as valid, but I emphasized other pastoral issues, such as character. Thus, after paying a high price for accepting the gifts, we lost much ground just by failing to continue to emphasize their importance.

In 1964 the issue that had gripped my life was the need for supernatural help, such as I saw in the New Testament. Death, disease, and demonic forces had made me see my spiritual impotence. Sure enough, after being baptized in the Holy Spirit, things began to happen. God had given me supernatural help in pastoral ministry.

I visited a lady in the psychiatric ward of a hospital who was an inactive member of our church. She had been an executive with a large retail store but developed problems with alcohol and emotional stress. When I talked with her, I made no mention of charismatic dimensions. I simply prayed for the Lord to help her. As I did so, I touched her on the shoulder. The power of God came on her. She became emotionally peaceful, and I left the room. A few days later she was at church, enthusiastically testifying to God's love and power toward her. She had been healed.

In the years that followed, my pastoral emphasis moved from counseling to prayer for supernatural help. We saw healings, deliverances from evil spirits, and manifestations of God's care on a regular basis. But I also saw gifts and ministries sometimes become carnival-like curiosities. Though I had often ministered in the power of the Spirit, I began to react to what I judged to be shallow, sensational, and a substitute for substance.

In 1973, my major emphasis became helping people live as members of God's kingdom, with the disciple relationship as the method of teaching the kingdom way of life. The lordship of Christ, obedience, serving, stewardship, honor for Christ and each other, and practical care for one another crowded out the more charismatic emphasis on evangelism, healing, and deliverance from evil spirits. While our groups never stopped praying for various supernatural manifestations and help, the emphasis became kingdom character and excellence. We would say, "Get it right before you try to give it to somebody else."

As a result of this shift in the early 1970s, our growth came from people who were looking for genuine friendship, training, pastoral care, and excellence of life. We did not always deliver, but these were things we taught. And we did grow. In three years, our church grew to over six hundred members locally, with hundreds more in other groups. In fact, within three years, I was indirectly responsible for over 2500 people. But by then, we were deep in controversy because of the pastoral emphasis that often seemed to be too controlling.

Another difficulty developed which we did not recognize

until 1980. We were developing a constituency that had not experienced the evangelistic and charismatic power that many of us had experienced in the 1960s. We realized a need to once again focus our people on the Holy Spirit and evangelism. We had been maturity oriented, but maturity cannot come apart from the practice of reaching out in the power of God. We had become so used to focusing on "getting it right" that we had almost stopped "getting it out."

Introspection and introversion are unhealthy. A preoccupation with personal development can lead to deterioration. Self becomes the cause. This happened to our movement to some extent in the late 1970s and early 1980s.

Seeing the problem, the other leaders with me began to stress the charismatic anew. Ern Baxter began to emphasize that the kingdom of God is in the Spirit; Bob Mumford began to focus on the supernatural; Derek Prince began to focus on miracles and evangelism. I taught on spiritual sensitivity and reproductivity. In our private counsels we had long and serious discussions over the true condition of our movement and the relationship between pastoral, governmental, and charismatic issues. By the early 1980s, we were attempting to restore charismatic and evangelistic qualifications for leadership alongside the qualifications of call, character and capacities. Again the charismatic dimension became an important criterion for leadership development.

According to Ephesians 4:10, pastors are a gift of the ascended Christ to the church. Pastoral ministry originates in the spiritual or supernatural realm. Pastoral leadership is Jesus Christ's ministry through men. As the God-man, Jesus Christ was not merely good, he was powerful. He not only cared about the suffering captives, he was able to deliver them. Extending his care, pastors must not only comfort and educate, they must deliver people from spiritual prisons by the power of God.

One does not pastor long before he comes face to face with insoluble situations. Our full-time and lay pastors were taught to give practical help for all the needs of the people in their care—financial, vocational, or whatever. Before long, they ran into needs that could not be met apart from the power of God. Were they equipped at that point? The question concerned us deeply as we assessed the state of the local church and broader movement.

In addition, we noticed that the person being cared for often looked on his pastor as "kingdom social security." It was as though the person asked himself, Why have insurance? My pastor and the church will help me. We discovered that some of our best efforts to care produced individuals who were more atuned to accepting a mothering process than learning spiritual fatherhood. They were too self-aware and therefore sensitive to offense. But true maturity comes from taking responsibility and becoming concerned for others. We desperately needed a renewed emphasis on evangelism. Were our leaders equipped at that point?

We had never lost a vision of Christ's kingdom affecting the whole world, but we had lost much of the practice of telling our neighbor. It was time to renew our emphasis on spiritual power and evangelism. By the mid 1980s, we began to conduct ministry training on evangelism and spiritual gifts. The power began to flow again, and our people began to become outward in their mentality.

First Corinthians 12 is one of several New Testament passages that deal with spiritual gifts, or charismata. The gifts are divine abilities flowing through human instruments. Since the gifts of the Holy Spirit are his, classifications and definitions are difficult, if not dangerous. There are as many gifts as there are ways the Holy Spirit chooses to act.

One vital area in which the Spirit acts is the *ministry of revelation and insight*. The word of wisdom, the word of knowledge, and discerning of spirits fall into the category of revelation gifts. Without the insight of the Holy Spirit, leaders are much like bus drivers speeding through the night without headlights. The passengers are trusting us to see as far ahead and around as possible. We can not afford to appoint leaders who do not seek and respond to the Holy Spirit's illumination of wisdom, knowledge, and evil spirits. Appointing blind leaders brings the responsibility for the subsequent collision on our heads.

Another vital area of Holy Spirit activity is the *power ministries*—faith, healing, and miracles. Jesus told his disciples, "You shall receive power after the Holy Spirit comes on you." The word for power there is *dunamis*. Dunamis is the same word from which we get words like dynamic or dynamite. Many Christians could think of almost any other adjective to describe what goes on in church besides the word dynamite.

The power of God is a blast! Jesus blew demons away with his authority. He healed paralytics. Healing can be powerful. It can blow doubt away! I was on the rostrum at a Katherine Kuhlman meeting in 1969 and I saw a woman with a withered hand healed. I saw the woman stretch out her knarled withered hand, and her hand was made whole! It was powerful!

Jesus cursed a fig tree and it died. That is also powerful. The disciples were amazed and Jesus said, "That's nothing. If you had a grain of faith you could throw a mountain into the sea!"

If Jesus had not had supernatural power, he could not have passed on his message. His works testified to the authenticity of his message. I wonder how long churches without the power of God will be able to pass along their message.

It is not God's intention that all of the miracles be done by famous individuals. The supernatural power of God is a gift of the Holy Spirit given to the body of Christ, the church. Unless leaders function in the power of God, they can not lead their people to function in the power of God. Unless they lead their people to function in the power of God, the church cannot lead the world to see the power of God and therefore believe the word of God.

A third vital area of the Holy Spirit's ministry is the area of *proclamation ministry*—prophecy, tongues, and interpretation of tongues. I believe Scripture is speaking of something supernatural, something more than learned verbal skills. These gifts are the abilities to deliver the message whether in a learned or unknown language. Or they may be the verbal means to express the desire of the Holy Spirit in prayer. Whatever one's view, it was a regular occurrence in the apostolic church. Anyone who aspires to lead God's people will need divinely inspired praying and preaching.

The charismatic movement has brought a fresh emphasis to the entire church on the whole subject of spiritual gifts. Currently the church is in the midst of a resurgence of spiritual gifts.

When I was baptized in the Holy Spirit in 1964, the Pentecostals were the only ones saying much about the gifts of the Holy Spirit. For the most part, their focus was primarily on the experience of being baptized in the Holy Spirit with the accompanying sign of speaking with tongues, rather than on all of the spiritual gifts. In recent years, however, that has changed. Not only are the Pentecostals speaking about other gifts, but so are Roman Catholics, Presbyterians, Episcopalians, Methodists, Baptists, and a whole host of other confessional and nondenominational churches. Many of the largest local church bodies in the world today are churches actively teaching and practicing the supernatural gifts of the Holy Spirit.

As an example of how things have changed, when I was preparing for the ministry through college and seminary, I do not recall one advocate of supernatural gifts as a tool for ministry. No one taught me how to exercise spiritual gifts, or even that I should. Today, however, thousands of teachers and advocates are telling potential leaders that they need the power of the Holy Spirit and his manifestations if they are going to fulfill the commission of the Lord.

Many pastors and Christians think that the gifts of the Spirit, if they exist at all, belong to an abnormal few. But Ephesians 4 clearly states that the pastors which Christ gives to the church assist the members of the body to function in the power of God so the church can be built up. Not only is it Christ's intention that his gifts be resident in pastors, but it is the duty of pastors to train all the members of the body to function in the power of the Holy Spirit and be active in exercising spiritual gifts. This is one of our greatest challenges. We must teach people how to recognize the presence of God, hear his voice, and obey his instructions. We must teach them how to know that they have heard the Spirit, how to confirm what they think they have heard. They need biblical foundations, subjective sensitivity, circumstantial evidence, and affirmation of leaders in order to identify which way the Holy Spirit is moving.

A dispensationalism which teaches us that Holy Spirit ministries ceased to be active after the death of the last apostle has performed more disservice to evangelical Christianity than any other single theological device. Not only is it unbiblical, but it has blinded millions of Christians to the knowledge of God's provision. God intends us to function beyond our natural abilities in the power of the Holy Spirit. The testimony of Scripture—"Without me you can do nothing"—still holds. It is contradictory to say, "I believe in the Bible," yet to also say, "The gifts are not for today," and it renders much of the Bible of no effect.

Once a man is recognized as a potential pastoral leader in the body of Christ, he should be given every opportunity to understudy with other leaders who have maturity in the ministries of the Holy Spirit. This is both the biblical and practical way to become effective in spiritual ministry.

I was twenty-seven years old when I was baptized in the Holy Spirit. I received a new motivation to serve the Lord Jesus and a new sense of spiritual power. But even with my Christian education and seven years of pastoral experience, I had never had one lesson on the place of speaking in tongues in the church or on interpretation of tongues. I had never had one lesson on the nature of the gift of prophecy or on how it should operate among members of the church. I did not even know how to pray for the sick. I did not know if everyone was supposed to be healed. I did not know if healing was provided for us in the atonement of Christ. I did not know how to respond if I prayed for someone and they did not get well. I did not know how to cast out a demon. The tragedy for me was that unlike many secularized Christians I believed in the existence of demons. But since I had never been taught how to cast them out, I was stuck with them. I was worse off than the theological liberals who denied them. The theological liberals could deny that they existed, but I had to live with my inability to deal with them.

According to the Bible, our enemy is in the supernatural realm. He is not flesh and blood. We will never be able to deal with him effectively until we become competent in the spiritual realm. Scripture is explicit as to how we can arm ourselves effectively and how we can even take the offensive against our spiritual enemy.

The church's future success depends on the kind of leaders we appoint. The older a leader gets, the more he looks to see who is coming along to receive what has been built. Moses had a Joshua. David had a Solomon. Jesus had the apostles. Who will we train?

Whoever we choose to succeed us will be entrusted with the people for whom Christ died and for whom we lived. They will need to know the call of Christ, develop the character of Christ, reach for the capacity to contain more of Christ, and move in the power of Christ—the Anointed One.

Part III:
Developing New Leaders

TEN

The Process

To UNDERSTAND ANY CHURCH MOVEMENT, it is necessary to understand the forces to which it is reacting. I reacted to two primary conditions as I saw them: the powerlessness of most denominational Christianity and the structurelessness of most charismatic Christianity. These reactions caused me to seek the power of God and the best structures for kingdom living. These reactions also caused some distortions in my view of the ministry and how to prepare for it.

My own training had been in family, church, college, and seminary. Because the formal educational institutions of the church had neglected the charismatic dimensions of training, I virtually rejected institutional training as an instrument for pastoral training. Instead, I focused on our local church, which had become charismatic, and on personal discipling as virtually the only instruments for training potential pastoral leaders.

In the early 1970s, as the new church began to develop, I began to give myself to relationships with emerging leaders. We stressed a discipling process of impartation by association and example. It offered some strengths that are missing from traditional ministry training, and it had some weaknesses that would have been supplied by traditional ministry training.

Teaching is often reduced to passing on of truth as

information. Training is the incarnating of truth in behavior through discipline.

Once a person comes to believe that he or she has a divine purpose, that person should begin to seek both practical and academic training. Unfortunately, institutional teachers often invite potential leaders to be taught without giving them a relationship to teachers or opportunity for practical application. Hence the new leader goes forth with knowledge but is often insecure, alone, and impractical. Teaching that only occurs in a classroom often only works in a classroom. Training that occurs in daily life works there.

Who can say when training begins or ends? If one accepts a sovereign redemptive God, then preparation begins with God's selection. Jeremiah was reminded he was chosen from the womb, and David wrote inspired words about the same truth. We must broaden our concept of training if we are to broaden our cooperation with God's purpose and plan. Even our earliest mistakes are fertilizer for future ministry. My earliest family memories are Christian and pastoral. Are those memories less valuable than the more formal learning processes of later years? I do not think so.

I and those with me, on the other hand, reacting against the shortcomings we had experienced in institutional training, invited potential leaders to relate to us. We took responsibility to help them to relate to people and situations where they could apply what they learned. But we often lacked sufficient curriculum and disciplines to equip them for their potential.

It became clear that these ingredients must come together: (1) Relationship to responsible and successful instructors, (2) Relationship to a real atmosphere of practical application in the church, and (3) A knowledge and power that truly equips.

One cannot study the writings of the apostle Paul, as he was moved by the Holy Spirit, without realizing that he was both inspired and educated. He studied at the feet of a prominent teacher of his day, was discipled in the rabbinical tradition, and was a Pharisee. While other disciples and apostles of the New

Testament may not have had as much formal training, it is clear that they had a good working knowledge of the Old Testament and the teachings of Jesus. Even as Jewish children they were taught tradition and Scripture to a degree that does not happen in most Christian homes.

While most of the disciples had little formal training, Jewish officials were impressed by their ability to give an account of their faith in the face of opposition. Jesus may have short-circuited some of the customary formal Jewish training, but his discipling proved even more effective. He succeeded in producing some powerful and knowledgeable leaders—and results are the best measure of a method of training.

When the apostle Paul ministered in Ephesus, he spent two years teaching the disciples daily. Not only did he teach them in the academic sense but he also taught them in the practical sense, performing many miracles among them, preaching, and teaching. This enabled the word of God to spread throughout all the region. Again, the effectiveness of his training methods were evident in the results. The apostle Paul did not separate the academic from the practical and the supernatural.

Timothy was told to study to show himself approved unto God, a workman who is not ashamed, rightly dividing the word of truth. He was further told to teach faithful men who would teach others.

Thus, the training process is demonstrated for us in several ways: Jesus' relationship with his disciples, the prolonged and intensive ways in which the apostle Paul and other apostles taught new leaders, and Paul's exhortation to Timothy to teach faithful men who would teach others.

It is important to bear in mind that training in Scripture does not merely produce academic expertise or an ability to recite facts. Biblical training was associated with proven leaders in the arena of task. It was practical and successful.

The Western approach to training is almost exclusively academic. This gives it an emphasis on theory and sometimes removes it from reality. Whenever training occurs in academic isolation, away from the arena of practical application, it is likely to produce a graduate who is unable to relate what he knows to what he needs to accomplish.

By contrast, New Testament training was associated with application. Jesus' classroom was a mobile demonstration of his convictions and principles. Acts 1:1 speaks of what Jesus began both to do and to teach. The doing came before the teaching. In modern teaching, it would probably be the reverse. Jesus' teaching came out of live situations and supernatural activity so it did not create mere idealism in the disciples, divorced from practical realities. Jesus' teaching enabled his disciples to do the kinds of things he did.

I have always enjoyed sports. When I was in high school, I enjoyed playing football. Four days a week we would do exercises, run plays, and scrimmage. Every Friday before the game we would not do any strenuous exercise or contact which might cause injury. Instead we had what the coach called "skull practice." We sat in a classroom, and the coach lectured us on the mental side of the game. He diagramed plays on the board and reminded us of the important aspects needed to win the game.

In most preparation for pastoral ministry today, about four days a week is "skull practice" and only one day or less is practice in a live situation. In some cases, skull practice consumes the entire training program and the candidate never actually gets out on the field to put into practice what has been learned—until he is thrust completely into the real situation. Then he is often alone.

As a young minister, I found myself pastoring and going to school at the same time. Doing both made me acutely aware of the shortcomings of a predominantly academic approach to preparing pastoral leaders. I was conscious of the fact that many of my teachers had never pastored growing churches. Some of my teachers did not seem to favor growing churches. Their teaching was often speculative and dealt with theological criticism. Much of what I heard in class was of little value to my ministry and, if taken seriously, could have been harmful, such as much of my training in secular psychology. High-sounding jargon and intellectual smugness rendered some of the professors incapable of communicating with ordinary people. It also rendered some students the same way. Sadly for many of them, their academic education was like Saul's armor which was offered to David prior to his battle with Goliath. David rejected the armor because it was unnatural to him, too unwieldly. Had he accepted the armor, he could not have defeated the giant. Many young Davids do accept a shallow notion of education that proves to be a liability, rendering them clumsy and off target.

In the New Testament, training was not an island in the sea of reality. It was usually associated with a local church. Teaching and mission were connected. I believe that one of the great changes we will see in ministerial training in the future is that it will become more closely related to local churches that are demonstrating the power of God and growing.

Training is for God's purposes, not for our professional perpetuation. Potential leaders, whether lay leaders or full-time clergy, need training in subjects such as theology, biblical languages, ecclesiology, homiletics, counseling, principles of scriptural interpretation, Christian history, and eschatology. Their training can be formal and specialized. But it needs to be identified with the task of discipling nations and to be offered in the context of churches that are attempting to do it.

The teachers should be those who are committed to a biblical worldview and will keep the faith with the Lord of the kingdom. The atmosphere should be that of a Christian community in which the leaders and teachers are functioning in the subjects at hand. And the power of God should evidence his presence and blessing.

If I were asked to evaluate the church and movement that I represent, I would say that in spite of our most sincere emphasis on discipleship, our greatest need is a training mechanism that fulfills the criteria that I have presented.

God views training as a vital responsibility, one that we will never do too well. Jesus took the training of the world's future leaders out of the hands of those who would merely reproduce religious copies and put it in the hands of those who were committed to the purposes of God. Unless our leadership training suits his purpose we will forfeit our opportunity to take the kingdom of God to the nations of the earth.

ELEVEN

Recognition

AS I LOOK BACK, I can see definite steps that led me toward being given the opportunity to pastor. The call of God became clear in 1955. I had tremendous battles over various issues the Lord raised with me—foul language, tobacco, lust, a pugilistic attitude, and arrogance, to name a few. After I accepted his call, my capacities and aptitudes were sorely tested by education and ministry situations that challenged me to grow and change.

I was not ready, but who is ever really ready? I obeyed God, and my Baptist pastoral superiors gave me recognition and ordination.

Subsequent to my ordination on December 1, 1957, I was privileged to participate in the ordination of several other Baptist pastors. They were men who testified to a call, had some degree of formal training, had been invited by a church to pastor, had been examined by a presbytery of ordained pastors, and were then presented by the presbytery before a congregation with the laying on of hands.

After fourteen years with Baptists, I found myself outside that traditional context, preparing other men to lead. Frankly, I was unprepared to deal with some significant issues regarding how a leader is trained and set into place for service. Often, however, the need does not wait for us to get prepared, and I soon found myself having to send leaders into service without a prescribed process for training or recognition. We had no idea that the church and the other groups I was relating to elsewhere would grow so fast and demand so much from leaders. Consequently, some of the leaders lacked the proper foundation.

These experiences have led me to some convictions about the process of formally recognizing leaders in the church. Any emerging leader, I have come to see, whether a lay pastor or a full-time pastor, who testifies to the call of God, should have his character, abilities, and gifts scrutinized by *proven Christian leaders* who will bear some ongoing responsibility for his service to the church. Upon their counsel, the potential leader should proceed with a process of training. In addition to preparing the person for leadership, the process should also demonstrate the nature of the candidate's commitment to Christ and the ministry. Then there should come a time to reevaluate the entire process before his actual ministry is launched. This reexamination is designed to confirm that the candidate was truly called. It should also confirm that his character and natural and spiritual abilities have been correctly assessed.

A presbytery, or council of leaders, may not be able to say that the leader was not called by God to some form of leadership. But they have the obligation to determine his ability to serve in the particular context for which they are responsible.

Reexamination and confirmation are designed to build a foundation of the church's confidence for his successful functioning in the future. It also strengthens the candidate's own confidence by giving him the approval of his peers. It strengthens his identity as part of a team of leaders, rather than as an isolated leader. It provides him with a plurality of counsel, resources, and spiritual gifts that will strengthen his future leadership. At the outset of his leadership, it teaches him that corporate approval or disapproval have a strong impact on his ability to function.

Ordination is a widely recognized form of recognition. Ordination means "to appoint or to set in order." A presbytery, or council of pastoral leaders, cannot make someone a man of God. Rather, they point out to the rest of the church that a certain man has been chosen by God to serve as a leader.

It has been my custom and the custom of the pastoral leaders from my religious background not to ordain a man until he is called by a particular congregation to function as their pastor. It has always seemed prudent to me to ordain a man at the point when his gifts have been recognized and he is ready to actually bear responsibility, rather than give him a ministerial status without ministerial responsibility. In the case of a lay pastor, he may be recognized in some manner when placed in responsibility over a group within a local congregation.

Ordination is a formal occasion where a recognized body of spiritual leaders, or presbytery, is convened to examine and publicly commission a newly emerging pastoral leader. In addition to recognition, ordination contains an impartation of spiritual power and authority which further enables the new leader to function.

There are at least seven elements in the ordination process:

1. A prepared candidate. The candidate should be one who is in personal relationship with the Lord, who has profound awareness of his conversion to Jesus Christ by the power of the Holy Spirit, who has a sense of calling to pastoral leadership, who has an adequate degree of training, who has a heart open to service, and who has Christian relationships with his family, his church, and his civic community.

2. A body of leaders who have been responsible for the training of the candidate, who are able to evaluate him, and who will take responsibility for his continuing performance.

3. An examination or dialogue with the leaders, or presbytery, in some way responsible for the candidate. Ordination or licensing should not be obtained without there being ongoing accountability. It is my view that the examination and ordination process should take place in the presence of ministers who have been responsible for the emergence of the candidate, if possible, and certainly in the presence of ministers who are going to take responsibility for the candidate's performance in the future.

4. A recommendation for ordination from the responsible presbytery to the church or ordaining body. In many circles the presbytery can examine, but authority for ordination rests with the local congregation. Under those circumstances, it is important that a local congregation not proceed with ordination until the one being ordained is approved by a group of peers who have experience in the ministry to which the pastoral candidate is called. I believe that that same body of pastoral leaders ought to be responsible in some way for the ongoing behavior and ministry of the one being ordained.

5. Appropriate admonitions and charges to the candidate to be faithful to God who has called him, to the word of God which is his message, and to the people of God to whom he is sent. If the ordination is done in the presence of the congregation, there should be charges to the congregation to treat the man of God in accordance with the Scripture and to uphold and support him as a servant of the Lord.

6. Prayer and spiritual ministry to the candidate, commending him to God and his word, reinforcing the gifts of God within him, and giving him any spiritual revelations or utterances from the Lord. The apostle Paul reminded Timothy to wage a good warfare by the prophecies which had gone on over him. Ordination should be a powerful time, further equipping the candidate to do God's will.

7. A commission to the ministry with full authorization of the presbytery and the church, with the recognition that the servant of God is God's own choice, authorized by God himself. The candidate should be given a mandate to extend the kingdom of God.

After the ordination, the pastor should have a sense that he is not merely the servant of the presbytery, the congregation,

making of home-groups leaders

or the denomination, but that he is first of all the servant of God. He should be so charged with the power and purpose of God that he would, if necessary, make any sacrifice.

These elements are applicable to formal or informal settings. They can be applied in some fashion to leaders of small groups in the church as well as senior pastors. It would be helpful if all leaders of care groups, house groups, and so on were examined, commended by the presbytery, prayed over in the presence of all, charged with the work of the Lord, and commended to the congregation with a solicitation from the congregation that they would be duly supportive.

In the future, I believe, more pastoral care will be delegated to members of the congregation. While they may not be called to full-time ministries, they are certainly called to care for the flock. Therefore, every step should be taken to recognize their call and encourage them in it. The health and power of the church in the future will depend on those who will stand with the senior pastors in the shepherding of the flock of God.

A weak process of confirming leaders can lead to a breakdown of effective leadership among the people. It is important to elevate the recognition process so that the ministry can be elevated and performed effectively. The presentation of new pastors should be handled in a way that would encourage others whom God is calling to the pastoral ministry and cause more young people to aspire to be called to the leadership of the church.

There seems to be a resurgence in the practice of honoring successful members of professions. People in the fields of entertainment and public service are being honored publicly for achievement and effectiveness. This is a good practice. We in the church must not forget that all honor proceeds from God. God himself honors his servants and honors his people who are faithful to him. The formal recognition of ministry provides the church with an opportunity to honor not only an individual but also to honor God. In addition, ordination and recognition give an occasion to honor one of the most necessary roles of service in the world—the calling to lead and care for the people of God.

While ministry recognition is a very serious matter, it can be a joyful celebration. Friends and family members can be invited to rejoice that God has raised up another leader who will continue the ministry of Christ and care for his people.

The responsibility to develop pastoral leaders who extend the care of Christ for his people is a great challenge to the entire church, and especially to its current leaders. How effectively we carry out this mission will determine how effectively the church carries out its mission. Considering that the church is the light of the world, developing strong pastoral leaders will have an impact on the whole world.

you don't lead by discouraging

leader needs to be open to other leaders

homegroup leaders approved by all the leaders and then recognized before the congregation.

He talks of a presbytery

He talks of training

pg. 91 meetings in which people can express their ideas.

Pastoral care goes on forever
Discipling does not go on forever.
Somebody who makes disciples, is
not being discipled anymore. But
you always stay <u>under</u> <u>authority</u>,
not just to one, to all other leaders.

Part IV:
Real Leadership

1. Do it for them
2. " " with them
3. Watch them do it
4. Release them

We need pastoring, simply meaning
care, but it is up to us to ask
for it or accept it. When it is used
as a form of control then it is wrong
Discipleship means being primarily young christians, — less and less
other mature christians — <u>they are
being released</u> <u>when they are firm in
Christ.</u> (all voluntary)

pastoral care therefore

He cannot excercise leadership in this atmosphere.

Mike Freeman should have come to Bert. Bert would have talked + Ron.

Bert was not involved until accusations had been made and everything had been decided.

I have been so discouraged from taking initiative by the angry outbursts, that I have been paralized.

pg. 117
118   opportunity to do whatever is in his heart

The leader ought to be consulted whether the home group leader should be the discipler or pastor.

I would like to try a ministry team on the alternate Wednesday (worship team) adult education bible study.

TWELVE

"The Shoot Out" Over Authority

I HAVE FACED TWO MAJOR SPIRITUAL WARS since going into the ministry. One was over the work of the Holy Spirit. The second was over the authority of spiritual leaders. Neither was academic. I moved into areas where I felt God was leading, and then came an explosion and conflict.

In retrospect, there was a lot I did not know about both subjects, and still do not know. Both are rooted in eternity. But progress only comes when we are willing to fail, indeed, when we would rather fail than to refuse to try to follow the Holy Spirit.

In 1964, I had an experience of God's love and power. Everything I knew about the Holy Spirit convinced me that it was from God. The experience was not a momentary encounter with the Spirit, but an entering into a new awareness of God's presence, initiative, and gifts for his church. To hold on to the word and power of God, I had to stand in opposition to everything around me that would deny it. The most intense wars are "holy wars." Mine was a war for existence and for the future shape of my ministry. It lasted several years, and there was little short of physical violence that was not used by my spiritual enemy to intimidate or destroy my ministerial credibility. I had not only to stand but also to do so in grace and love. I had to become strong, stronger than I wanted to be.

However, during those years from 1964 to 1971, I continued to lead Bay View Heights Baptist Church. The conclusion of the battle was not that I won, but that I survived. After the battle, my leadership was stronger. We had elders, and I sought council from them, but there was no question who led the church. C. Peter Wagner says in his book, *Your Church Can Grow*, that the pastor is the key to growth. He points out that the great and growing churches of America have strong pastors. The title of one chapter is "Pastor, Don't Be Afraid of Power." While recognizing the importance of spiritual gifts and a corporate approach to leadership, Wagner points out the importance of the pastor being willing to exercise leadership.

However intense the battle for the validity of charismatic power was, it was not nearly as intense and painful as the battle over spiritual authority. I was better prepared for my denomination's reaction to the gifts of the Spirit than I was to the charismatic renewal's reaction to authority.

The issue of spiritual authority, and especially pastoral authority, caused a major controversy in the charismatic renewal in the mid 1970s. Here is some of what occurred. In 1973, Dick Coleman, who was a pastor in central Florida, invited me to lead a pastors' conference. We agreed to invite all men who were leading any kind of Christian church or group—lay pastors or full-time pastors—to deal with the issues in pastoral ministry. We called it a "shepherds' conference" because the term seemed inclusive of all those we were inviting. To our surprise, over four hundred pastors and other leaders showed up. It was an amazingly powerful meeting that lasted several days. The men who took part were predominantly nondenominational, if not anti-denominational, leaders in the charismatic renewal.

The next year, several pastor friends and I put on another conference at Montreat, North Carolina, which 1,500 attended. It was even more powerful than the one the year before. Derek Prince, Ern Baxter, Don Basham, Bob Mumford, John Poole, Jim Moore, Steve Clark, Ralph Martin, and myself were some of the leaders. The worship released a great thunder of power and praise.

Pastors and other leaders were desperate for brotherly relationships and spiritual authority in their lives. Hundreds of them made commitments to one another for care and mutual edification.

In 1975, we sponsored another conference. This time we went to Kansas City and nearly 5,000 leaders met together, with the same kinds of results. We continued to call the meeting a "shepherds' conference," inviting all kinds of lay and full-time pastors to come together and examine pastoral issues. A large number of the men could be referred to as lay pastors with small groups. By no means were all of those leaders committed to myself or the other conference leaders. They were there to hear and see what the Lord was saying about pastoring.

Some of us had begun to encourage stronger pastoral leadership over congregations. We had begun to use the shepherd model as a serious example of how pastors should relate to their people. Derek Prince wrote a short book entitled *Discipleship, Shepherding, and Commitment* that sketched how submission to pastoral leadership should work.

What followed the Kansas City shepherd's conference of 1975 was a firestorm of controversy. Many charismatic renewal leaders felt that some of us who led the shepherds' conference were trying to take over the charismatic movement. Others cited some of our teaching to confirm that we wanted authority. *Christianity Today* erroneously reported that we called ourselves apostles. The charges are too numerous to list here.

Some leaders with cooler heads suggested that we have a reconciliation meeting that would be unannounced and by invitation only. We expected about twenty to twenty-five leaders to gather at the Curtis Hotel in Minneapolis.

When I arrived at the meeting, scheduled for early afternoon, the room was running over with uninvited men. Blood pressures were high, affidavits, tape recordings and accusations were everywhere. It took about three hours to clear the room of the uninvited. What followed was something less than a peaceful ecumenical council. I can now laughingly call it "the shoot out at the Curtis Hotel." (Later the Curtis Hotel was torn down. I thought it might happen that day.) We met for two days trying to achieve harmony, but there was no reconciliation in some quarters. I scarcely slept during those nights and would have left the entire scene had not my brothers prevented me.

When Peter Wagner says, "Pastor, don't be afraid of authority," I understand what he means, but I would advocate a healthy respect for it.

After the meeting, I ran into various accounts of what happened in Minneapolis, largely from people who were not there and did not really know. They too had gotten caught in the furor of the spiritual war that we were all caught in. The battleground? Authority.

For the next three or four years, numerous books and articles appeared concerning the issue of how much authority pastors should have. Some centered in the Scripture and historical Christianity, but most just muddied the water.

We scrapped any future plans for shepherds' conferences because they no longer served the unity of the church. Instead, we went to work with denominational and nondenominational leaders to have a large general conference in Kansas City the following year. The result was an interdenominational conference in Kansas City that drew more than 50,000 Christians involved in the charismatic renewal across the churches in the United States and abroad.

To show our love for the rest of the church and our desire for unity, we were able to bring 9,000 people in our movement to the conference. That was second only to the Catholics, who had 17,000 there. The rest were Lutherans, Methodists, Baptists, Mennonites, and others. It was a grand conference and did something to help the charismatic climate, which had deteriorated. But the conference further confirmed that the "shepherding movement" was not understood by nondenominational folks in the charismatic renewal. Many of them would not participate in the ecumenical Kansas City conference because we were invited. Tensions were so high that when the conference committee hired a writer to produce a book on the conference, he left us out of the book because he was personally opposed to us. Even though we were such a large contingent of those there and originally guaranteed a large part of the budget, we were excluded from the official history of the conference because of the hostility of the writer.

This typified what was happening to us. Feelings were strong. The authority issue was not easily resolved.

It would have been simple if it were a purely academic or theoretical issue. But questions of government and authority are primary universal issues. Jesus was crucified over his claim to be king. The future of creation is involved, as well as the lives of people.

Serious abuses of authority have occurred, both inside and outside the church. Many people become uncomfortable when the word authority is mentioned. Certainly everywhere that authority is exercised this side of Christ's throne, human frailty enters in.

The big shoot out was not really at the Curtis Hotel. It has always been going on. The war is in us, as our spiritual enemy appeals to the worst in us, to use our opportunities for authority for personal advantage and self-serving, or to tempt us to throw off all authority and do only what is right in our own eyes.

Authority is not an issue we can duck. Christ rules; we rule with him. The question is how we can rule without ruin.

Society without rule and authority is an impossibility. When

Moses sought to deliver Israel with his stick by smiting an Egyptian, his own people asked, "Who made you ruler over us?" It took him forty years to be able to answer that question. By the time he was able to answer it, he did not want to. But because he did answer, Israel began to become a nation that could reflect the ways of God.

THIRTEEN

Strong or Weak Pastoral Leaders?

WHETHER OR NOT WE WILL HAVE STRONG PASTORAL LEADERS in the church will not be decided here. They must decide themselves. And they must decide in the time of testing. If they become strong it will not be because someone suggested it or because the church voted them to be; it will be because they know their call from God and have the confidence to stand through difficulties. But my prayer is that God's servants will display strength in leadership, not in opposition to the church but for the sake of it.

Israel had some of the great leaders of history who brought them through some of the great trials of history. Israel was never stronger than its leaders. The church has had its leaders. It has never risen above the leadership of those who are called up and out to the purpose of God. When Moses ordained Joshua he said be strong and courageous. Later, God said the same thing to Joshua three times.

David Abshire has written in the *Washington Quarterly*, "The stakes are high, for leaderless societies quickly lose their vision and sense of destiny and eventually succumb to the forces of listlessness" (Winter 1983). Abshire quotes Abraham Zaleznik, who finds that American business suffers from an excess of managers and a shortage of leaders. Leaders,

Zaleznik says, use organization to pursue goals that are important to them, while managers tend to be passive and preoccupied with structure and process.

Edward N. Luttwak makes the same point about the American military in his book *The Pentagon and the Art of War*. The military, according to his critique, suffers from an overabundance of bureaucracy and is overloaded with officers in management. It lacks a direct leadership dynamic between the commander and the soldier in the field. Luttwak charges the various branches of military with having more interest in expanding their budgets than serving the overall cause.

Could the same point be made about the church? Is it possible that men of God have fallen into the mode of management, as opposed to aggressive leadership? Is it possible that the church is waging war by committee and that the self-interests of various branches of the service have eroded our commitment to the Lord's commission? I think so.

While we must provide against tendencies to abuse strong leadership, we cannot let the fear of abuse negate leadership. To do so is to expose ourselves to another evil equally as bad—to become wanderers in some wilderness until a whole generation dies.

Strong leadership in the church is the opposite of self-serving leadership. It means that the pastor's strength is used to serve the members of the church rather than the pastor's own interests. The strong Christian leader bends all his efforts to see that the people in his care are growing in the knowledge of God's love for them and in their love for God. Strong leadership does not mean arrogant leadership. It means leadership geared to service.

One of the most powerful lessons in the spirit of service that I ever received came from a man who had no position of leadership. But his attitude was exactly the attitude that every leader should aspire to have.

I was invited to preach in a congregation that was predominantly black. I was to preach several times a day for several days. The congregation was so receptive that I preached with more zeal than usual. Since it was summer, I was thoroughly soaked with perspiration after each message.

At the first session I noticed a dapper, smiling gentleman who always tagged along within earshot but was never obtrusive. After a while I realized it was his task to be my special servant. He seemed so honored to help in any way that I allowed him to do things that I would normally do for myself, such as carry my Bible. What made it especially difficult for me to accept his help was that he was older than me. I thought he must be in his sixties. Later I discovered he was close to eighty.

After concluding a particularly vigorous message, I retired to the pastor's lounge. I started to take off my jacket.

"Wait, you can't do that!"

I turned and saw this same gentleman in the lounge with me. His words made me think that I had violated some unknown taboo. He seemed upset.

"What do you mean?" I asked.

"You can't do that because that's my job." He began helping me take my jacket and shirt off, handing me a dry towel and some cologne.

"You see," he continued, "The Lord could not come in person, so he sent you. You are a messenger from God! I can't preach. I wish I could, but I'm not called to do that. But I can serve. That's my job. Oh, if the Lord would come in person, there's so much I would do. But he didn't come himself, he sent you. So I'm going to help you. You are a man of God!"

Tears welled up in my eyes. He was serving me as unto the Lord. I was humbled in his presence.

Finally, he finished helping me with my tie and jacket as he concluded his message on serving by saying, "My, you look nice!"

I will never forget being taught the art of serving by that great man. His name, incidentally, was Brother Love. It is not mere coincidence that I had as much freedom to preach there as any place where I had ever preached. Their receiving me as the Lord's servant freed the Lord to bless them richly.

If churches had as great respect for the pastoral office as that church did, they would find that the Lord would work powerfully through those who occupied the office. Jesus told Israel they would not see him again until they learned to say, "Blessed is he who comes in the name of the Lord" (Mt 23:39).

And if pastoral leaders took on that man's spirit of service, they would gain the confidence and support of their constituents for strong leadership.

A pastoral leader should serve. He should be secure enough in his calling and character to be able to serve his constituents, if necessary even in menial ways. Serving demonstrates that he clearly understands that spiritual authority is not based on the trappings of power but on the divine substance of calling and gifting within him. He must also be able to accept service from his people as unto the Lord.

For both pastor and people, serving is the posture for learning. When one humbles himself to serve another, he or she is in the position of looking upward. Thus the position of serving is the same position as that of learning.

Given that leaders in the church should exercise leadership in a spirit of service, and have maturity and the oversight of other leaders, we should all pray that they will be strong and courageous instead of being reduced to mere managers.

Here are some of the reasons:

1. Pastoral leadership should be strong because it comes from Christ. Ephesians 4:10-11 teaches us that pastors are gifts of the ascended Christ to the church. Recognition of that fact means that we receive the pastor as sent from God. If a pastor and people do not believe that, then there is in fact no basis for him to function in leadership.

2. Pastoral leadership should be strong because it oversees the church. Pastors are overseers. In Acts 20:28, the apostle Paul tells the elders, who are shepherds, to oversee or "bishop," the flock. Pastors cannot oversee from under the pile of people and duties. If a person is not *over,* he cannot *see* over. The fact that Jesus served did not lessen his role as chief overseer, and the fact that pastors serve does not lessen their role as overseers. People who do not want strong pastors do not want oversight.

3. Pastoral leadership should be strong because it leads people into God's purpose. Groups do not get visions, leaders do. Shepherds are leaders. That is obvious by the nature of the metaphor. A shepherd does not drive the sheep, he goes before them. It was a mistaken pastor who said, "There go my people, and I'm their leader."

Hebrews 13:7 reminds us to remember those who lead us, who speak the word of God to us. It exhorts us to consider their conduct and imitate their faith. It is an admonition to follow spiritual leaders.

Of course, we should not follow blind leaders. If we have reason to believe that our leaders are not people of vision, who see God's purpose, then we should be elsewhere.

4. Pastoral leadership needs to be strong because it accounts to God for the people. Hebrews 13:17 clearly tells the church to submit to and obey leaders because they watch for the souls of the people and give an account to God. The warning is that if the pastoral leaders, who are sent by God, give a bad report to God, it is not good for the church.

There is no doubt in my mind that many churches are not prospering because they have dishonored their leaders—past or present.

I remember on one occasion praying for various people I had on my list. The Lord spoke to me and said, "You have some on your list that are not on mine, and I have some on mine that are not on yours." I realized that my sense of accountability needed to be adjusted to coincide with my spiritual assignments. I believe stubbornness and rebellion can put people in a place where God assigns no one to watch for their souls.

5. Pastoral leaders should be strong because they must

correct the wayward member. Paul told Timothy to correct (2 Tm 4:2). Paul himself demonstrated a willingness to correct.

On one occasion the Lord rebuked me because I did not confront a brother about a fault. The Lord showed me that I did not love my brother enough to risk his anger and disapproval. It takes more love to correct than to remain passive. It also takes courage and strength. Many people do not appreciate even the most loving correction. A pastor whose leadership is weak will not be severe enough to correct. Discipline has been out of style. But it will return.

6. Pastoral leaders should be strong because they must stand between the people and danger. In Psalm 23, John 10, and other passages, we have the picture of the shepherd putting his life on the line for the people. The hireling runs away, but the true shepherd stands at the risk of his life.

David killed the lion and bear who threatened the flock, and the giant who threatened Israel. He was a man after God's heart. He was strong and put his life on the line. Jesus died in our place. He took the blows meant for us.

Weak leaders will not take the blows. They will not face lion, bear, or giant. Once self-interested dynamics have destroyed their confidence, they will leave the flock to the wolves when it becomes dangerous to stay.

7. Pastoral leadership should be strong because it represents Christ to the world. First Timothy 3:7 says that an overseer must have a good reputation among those outside the church. The leader of any unit of people is their representative and establishes their reputation outside.

Usually, our concern for the reputation of the church focuses on the ethics and goodness of the leaders. But reputation is also related to the strength of the leaders. A major reason that strong pastoral leadership is often correlated with large churches, as C. Peter Wagner and others have found, is simply because people are attracted to strong leadership. The kind of leadership a church has will determine its attractiveness to a world that needs godly leadership.

While I can think of many more reasons for strong, bold leadership, I cannot think of one for weak leadership. Nameless, faceless, or timid leadership has no biblical precedent that might offer hope. To the contrary, one might think of Abraham's nephew, Lot, of Eli or of Saul—men who meant well but lacked the courage to act or discipline. Or worse, one may think of Pilate, who could not decide to follow his conscience.

Weak leaders falter in the crisis and forfeit the trust in the pastoral office won by nobler hands in other days.

Strong leadership does not mean ignoring the wisdom that the Spirit communicates through the whole membership of the church. It does mean disregarding the opinions of others. Strong leaders have the personal security to listen to others' view when they are different from their own. Wise pastoral leadership will develop mechanisms for keeping in touch with where all the members of the church are. Among these are house groups, lay leaders, and meetings in which people can express their ideas.

Strength is not insecurity translated into defensiveness, or selfishness. It is not arrogance or harshness. It is not abuse or patronizing behavior. It is not macho bragging or bravado. It is not a swaggering gait or cynical laughter. It is not taking advantage of another's weakness.

Strength is knowing the faithfulness of God and the blood covenant in Christ. Strength is knowing that we are still standing when others thought we had long since fallen. Strength is knowing that we have nothing except that which has been given by the mercy of God. Strength is knowing when to admit our weakness and how to defer to the Holy Spirit. Strength is confessing the unalterable word of God, when we have nothing to say for ourselves. Strength is loving not our own lives, even unto death.

Pastoral leaders will either learn to be strong in the Lord and the power of his might, or they will settle into the path of least resistance, which makes man and rivers crooked.

Part V:
Disciple-Making

FOURTEEN

Who Should Make Disciples?

THE ISSUE OF STRONG PASTORAL LEADERSHIP leads to another issue: disciple-making. Strong pastoral leadership inevitably draws learners who want to know both the successful servants of God and how they have been successful. The servant of God, whatever his specific call, must then know what to do with this God-given influence.

In 1971 Derek Prince, Don Basham, Bob Mumford, and I were teaching a six-week seminar in the Washington, D.C., area. I was absent from one of the planning sessions. Derek suggested that I teach a three-message series on Discipleship, Fellowship, and Worship. When I met again with the other teachers, I was a bit put out because I had been assigned three subjects on which I had done little teaching. In fact, I had never taught on discipleship per se.

As I began preparing for the sessions, I wondered why I had not taught on those subjects before. They were primary biblical subjects. The Great Commission, which I had preached on many times before, was specifically about making disciples. As I reviewed the disciple-making of Jesus, the whole subject made a profound impact on my life and ministry. I also realized that I had been engaged in the process of discipling.

The Greek words translated "disciple" in the New Testa-

> Shepherding is what the Leader does. Disciples are learners. Do you ever stop being learners?

ment are various forms of the word *manthanō*. It means to learn. Disciples are learners. *Manthanō* is used some 25 times in the New Testament. *Mathētēs*, a disciple, is used more than 250 times in the New Testament. John's disciples are referred to 10 times, and Paul's 4 times.

Discipleship was used in the general sense to denote all of the followers of Jesus. "Christian" became interchangeable with the word disciple at Antioch (Acts 11:26). Disciple was also used specifically to denote those who learned the ways of Jesus from a particular teacher, such as from Paul or from Jesus himself.

The apostles were commanded to go and make disciples of all nations; Paul made disciples; women are exhorted to "learn" from their husbands (same word as be discipled); and Timothy was told to teach faithful men who could teach others. It would seem, therefore, that it was normal for New Testament leaders to be discipled and to make disciples. And though all Christians are primarily followers of Christ, it is normal for them to learn to follow Christ from some human agent who has himself learned to do so.

Christian discipleship is being under tutelage to learn the ways and ministry of Christ. It is the process of turning aliens and immigrants into solid citizens of the kingdom of God. It is not unlike the apprenticeship practiced in the trades and arts where skills are developed under the tutelage of a master craftsman. The notion of discipling is transvocational and transcultural. While there are many forms of discipling, it is always basically one person teaching another how to do something.

The purpose of discipleship is not to permanently fix someone in a relationship of subordination but to prepare the person for true fellowship and usefulness. Nor is it intended to produce carbon copies but rather to release the divine purpose hidden in the heart of the learner.

The church faces a major responsibility toward a person who has been converted to Jesus Christ. It cannot assume that the new birth or commitment to Christ that the person has made has automatically erased the secular educational processes that have formed that person. We must assume that through family background, education, entertainment, and other channels, the new convert has already been thoroughly influenced by a self-oriented society. We must therefore accept the responsibility placed on us by the Lord to thoroughly reeducate that new Christian with biblical values, Christian practice, the Holy Spirit's work, and a sound worldview. Discipleship can play a key role in this process.

Pastoring and discipling are not synonymous. Ezekiel 34, Jeremiah 23, and other passages teach us that the pastor's main responsibilities are to care, feed, lead, and protect. In my estimation, the word care best describes a pastor's ministry to his people.

When one genuinely cares, however, he attracts a special love and devotion from his constituents. This love enables him to go beyond caring to influencing and training for particular service. Pastors are in a unique position, therefore, to disciple and train young Christians. If pastors heed the exhortation to do the work of an evangelist (2 Tm 4:5), they should constantly be presented with new converts who need and desire personal training. Indeed, if they fail to disciple and train them, or to get others to do so, they are being poor stewards of the gifts God has entrusted to them. Evangelism should lead to discipling. The commission of the Lord is to disciple as well as evangelize.

It is important not to take out of context Jesus' general command to his disciples to make disciples and to apply his command indiscriminately to anyone who chooses to be a teacher. It is important to examine the qualifications of one who is attempting to make disciples. We must remember that Jesus spent three and a half years with his disciples before giving them personal approval to make disciples. He could commission them to make disciples because he knew that he had prepared them to do it. There are several factors that should be considered before one assumes the role of a discipler:

1. Approved. Any leader who disciples others should himself be approved by the spiritual authority to which he submits. The leader's spiritual overseers should also be willing to take some responsibility for the quality of the work he accomplishes. A discipler should not be a novice Christian.

Disciple-making is not a unilateral act. It proceeds out of the corporate approval of the body of leaders giving spiritual oversight. This is only right since the church will have to live with the result.

2. Under Authority. In Matthew 8, Jesus encounters a centurion whose servant is sick. The centurion requests that Jesus "speak the word" and his servant will be healed. The centurion recognizes Jesus' authority and realizes that Jesus would not have to go physically to pray for his servant, but that just a word would be sufficient.

It is interesting that the centurion did not say, "I also *have authority*." He said, "I am also *under authority*. Therefore, when I say to servants 'go,' they do." The centurion points out for us a basic principle: Those who *have* legitimate authority are those who are *under* legitimate authority.

As a pastor and member of a body of elders, I have sometimes been involved in ordination of a minister, only to discover later that he was failing to exercise his authority in a qualified manner. In some instances, it became necessary to seek the person's removal from the office. This was done to protect those who were under his care, as well as to protect the whole principle of pastoral leadership. The greatest harm to pastoral leadership comes not from those who oppose it from without but from those who abuse it by mismanagement. Pastoral leaders, therefore, need peers to whom they are accountable and who will take responsibility for correcting abuses. I would not advocate a disciple to be trained by someone who was accountable to no one.

3. A Servant's Attitude. The apostle Paul draws attention to the house of Stephanas, which he says was "addicted" to the work of the ministry. He exhorts the Christians in Corinth to submit to leaders like Stephanas. Stephanas had a track record and a right motivation that qualified him to receive people who needed discipling and pastoral care. Pastors who make disciples need to have a proven record of serving others. In my experience one of the chief dangers in any exercise of authority is using authority for personal gain. A servant's attitude will prevent that.

A pastor or lay pastor who is under the authority of the church leadership should be reminded that those he disciples are a trust, not a possession. A proprietary attitude—"These are *my* disciples"—is the beginning of domination and abuse of authority. All we have is given to us. A steward's mentality will keep a leader in a caring mentality instead of self-serving mentality.

4. Mature and Trained. Any would-be leaders who embark on the course of discipling others need to be mature and trained themselves. Nothing is more dangerous than a novice exercising authority and leading where he or she has not been.

My father tells a story about a sergeant who was very angry at a boot-camp trainee. The sergeant said to the trainee, "You idiot. I've taught you everything I know, and you still don't know anything." The truth of the matter is that much of the failure of those who are taught can be directly traced to the lack of experience on the part of the teacher. The teacher will be more equipped to serve if he has been through the process himself. It will enable him to understand the vulnerabilities of the disciple and the dynamics of the process, and he will not be as likely to be heavy-handed or insensitive with the disciple.

5. Spiritually Sensitive. While there are parallels between Christian discipleship and other forms of training, it must be completely clear that Christian discipling is a spiritual process. It cannot be duplicated by natural discipline. The kingdom of God is at its root a spiritual operation under the direction of the Holy Spirit. Natural discipline may be helpful, but spiritual discipline is the issue in Christian discipleship.

Jesus is the best example of discipling. The quality that stands out, beside his moral perfection, is his spiritual sensitivity. In exercising his leadership he was always sensitive to the Father. He did not view his role unilaterally but in total cooperation with the Father. He said, "What I do is what I see the Father doing. What I say is what I hear the Father saying." The disciples knew they were not being handled arbitrarily but were being handled in cooperation with the Father.

Spiritual sensitivity is an absolute must for any who seek to make disciples. It enables the leader to work with the disciple's own volition and ability to hear from God. A leader who does not allow his constituents to hear from God will produce followers who cannot hear from God. Ultimately the followers will become mechanical and spiritually dependent on their leader. A spiritually dependent person will remain unproductive.

6. Loving God's People. The one discipling must love the learners. First John 3:16 describes what love really means—Jesus Christ laid down his life for us. Therefore, we ought to lay down our lives for one another. To disciple requires laying down our lives.

Laying down one's life may not mean death, but it certainly means practical self-denial. It may mean death on the "installment plan"—dying daily. To disciple requires laying down self-serving things we could be doing with our talents. We lay down certain ambitions and personal glory in order to engage in elevating those under our care. Our investment is in others rather than ourselves. Discipling should be done with deep love, just as Christ laid down his life for his disciples and for us. Jesus Christ invested himself in the well-being of his followers.

After the resurrection Jesus asked Peter three times if he loved him. Each time Peter said yes. Each time Jesus told him to prove his love by caring for the lambs or feeding the sheep. The highest evidence that one loves the Lord is loving and caring for his people. This is the only acceptable motivation for making disciples. The biggest challenge, it seems to me, is not to die for Jesus; it is to die to myself in order to care for his people. I could see dying for Jesus—but some of his people? But to the Lord, each one is precious.

7. A Corporate Mentality. Isolation in disciple-making is a bad sign. In Acts 20:29-30 the apostle Paul warns the elders of the church in Ephesus that after he left some would arise from among them and draw away disciples after themselves. The problem here is not that some would rise up and make disciples. They were all expected to do that. But Paul warned them that whenever anyone drew the disciples away from the body of the church, it would tend to divide the body of Christ and produce aberrant disciples. Schism and perversion go hand in hand.

When the biblical qualifications for making disciples are ignored, bad things can happen. The Jim Joneses of history, the introverted cultic groups, the groups that produce serious perversions of the faith are not the results of true spiritual authority but of perverted authority. The qualifications for making disciples, and the proper kind of accountability in the ongoing leadership of God's people, are necessary to healthy discipleship. In 1985, I published a public apology through *New Wine* magazine because I felt that my teachings had been misused on some occasions. I felt I had not sufficiently guarded the truths of authority and that abuses had occurred. Disciple-making without accountability and a corporate mentality should be considered intolerable in the church for biblical and historical reasons.

Pastors need to see discipleship in both the broad and narrow sense. They need to be aware that all of their ministry is in a certain sense a discipling effort, teaching the people of God the ways of Jesus Christ. But they ought to go beyond this general kind of discipleship and practice personal discipleship with those that the Lord sends them, in order to raise up new leaders and teach faithful men who can teach others (2 Tm 2:2).

As a pastor discharges his responsibility to make disciples, he will be constantly reminded that he needs to meet in his own life the standards he is calling others to. Discipling will press a pastor closer to God and dependency on him. Pastors who obey the Lord in disciple-making will enjoy the fruit of spiritual fatherhood and reproductivity. They will also enjoy the commendation of the Lord who has commissioned us to make disciples.

Many writers and groups have sought to deal with the challenge to disciple. Among them are Robert Coleman, whose book *The Master Plan of Evangelism* is one of the best works on the subject. Another group which has pioneered the subject is the Navigators (P.O. Box 6000, Colorado Springs, CO 80934). In attempting to implement the ministry of discipling one would be well-advised to consult a variety of Christian groups or leaders who are committed to the process and have some experience with it.

FIFTEEN

How Discipleship Happens

SEVERAL YEARS AGO I drove a rental car from Anaheim, California, to the Los Angeles International Airport. While I had previously made the trip as a passenger, it was my first time to drive there. My wife, Carolyn, was helping me read the map as I drove north on a fast-moving, six-lane freeway. I knew the general direction of the airport. But after we had driven longer than should have been necessary, I realized we were passing Los Angeles altogether.

No problem; we had lots of time. I pulled off on an exit and stopped beside another driver at a red light.

"How do I get to the Los Angeles International Airport?"

"Turn around, go south, take the next freeway right, go several miles . . . you can't miss it."

We turned and went south, took the next right, and I drove several miles—no airport. It was getting dark now. There was less time. "Maybe I can follow the direction of the airplanes and see where the airport is." But following airplanes did not work either.

I got off the freeway again. "Maybe a service station operator can tell me the way." The area looked dark. I pulled into a station. "Sir, can you . . . ?"

He answered in Spanish.

"Does anyone else . . . ?"

"No speak English." We were in a hispanic area. This time I really had missed it!

Time was short. We drove down the deserted streets of a warehouse district. "I hope we don't have car trouble," I thought. "If only I had not assumed that I knew the way!"

Eventually, we came to a major street and stopped at a light.

"Can you tell me how to get to the Los Angeles International Airport?" I asked another motorist.

"Follow me!" he said, and he took off as though he knew I was late.

I did not know the man. How could I be sure that he knew the way? One thing was certain: I did not. I stayed on his bumper. He turned; I turned. He ran a yellow light; I ran a red one. Never have I clung to a moving relationship like I did that one.

After nearly ten minutes of turning, speeding, stopping, and starting again—there it was, the gate to Los Angeles Airport! It looked like heaven.

"Thanks," I yelled as he drove off. As soon as we boarded the plane, the doors closed behind us.

"Follow me," is what he had said. Others had pointed the way, but he led.

I reflected on that experience. You can miss it. Many people point, but some lead. They take the time to go out of their way and lead the person who has never made the journey before.

That is what Jesus did. He found the wanderers and said, "Follow me; I will take you there." That, in essence, is discipleship.

No matter how conscientious we are to form the disciple, however, and lead them to their destiny, we cannot assume total responsibility for success or failure. The disciple has a free will and is a priest unto God. The Holy Spirit enters into the process and must finally determine the potential of the disciple. The disciple is the Lord's.

The goal of discipleship is to impart the wisdom, character, and gifts of Christ to the learner and help the learner to find their call in Christ. Impartation is simply transferring one's own spiritual resources, including the Holy Spirit's resources, to someone else. The result is formation, not just information.

Discipleship is not something that we do *to* a disciple; it is something that we do *with* a disciple. Our responsibility is to represent Christ, be an example, and give what we can. But after evening prayers—go to sleep. Let the word do the work.

All of this is done in the hope that he or she will become productive and able to reproduce the process in the lives of others.

In 1973 I moved from Fort Lauderdale to the Mississippi Gulf Coast. I moved into the area for several reasons. One, to slow down my life and give myself to the issue of discipling. Secondly, I had groups in the area with whom I had worked in the past, and these people were supportive. After months of seeking the Lord, it became clear that that was where he wanted me to be. Whenever I gathered with my friends there, the presence of God seemed exceptionally powerful.

I began to relate to specific men in the area with a view to practicing Christian discipleship and helping bring them further into the purpose of God. Though I had begun to disciple earlier, there was a definite reprioritization, making discipleship more vital to my own life.

The Lord had been good to me. I had a good Christian family background and a reasonably good education (as much as I would receive). I had had fourteen years of pastoral experience, and some rather dramatic spiritual experiences, and I had traveled and preached in all kinds of groups in many nations. I also had a godly and attractive wife and three children whom we loved. I had been fulfilled. What I wanted was to impart what I could to whomever the Lord would send to receive it.

It would be inaccurate to give the impression that these were new relationships. In fact, I had worked with Glen, John, Terry, and others before. I had pastored and discipled them for several years. The same was true of Guy, Bob, Jerry, Horace, and others. But now we wanted to more clearly define and further explore what discipling and pastoring meant. Also I wanted to help them become more productive. They all became full-time pastors.

My efforts with these men were not typical of how discipleship normally begins. To look at how the relationship might ordinarily start, let's set up a hypothetical case.

Suppose I have pastored Vincent for the past five years. I baptized him in water on his conversion, and he has sat under my ministry. Vincent has been faithful, but he has never really developed in the Christian life. Then one day the Holy Spirit begins to show him that God has a greater purpose for his life.

In response to this, he comes forward after the service and says, "Brother Charles, I believe God is calling me to something. I'm not sure what it is. Can you help me find the will of God for my life?"

Also suppose that I have been watching Vincent for a number of months and was aware of God's hand on his life. I believed him to be sincere and hungry for spiritual things. I also saw in him the potential to influence other people's lives.

"Vincent, why don't you come by and visit with me this week? We can talk about your question and see what the Lord would say to us."

"Yes, I'd be glad to do that."

So Vincent comes by. In the meantime both of us have been praying.

"Vincent, I've been thinking about something. I wonder if you would like to have us spend time together so that I could help you find the purpose of God. It's been on my mind that the Lord has something for you. And as your pastor, I have a responsibility and desire to help you."

"Yes, that sounds good to me. I've often wanted to meet with you to ask questions about the sermons and what I think the Lord is saying to me. But I've been hesitant, since I know you're a very busy person."

"I'm glad to hear you say that, Vincent, because I have it in my heart to spend some time with you. However, I did not want to force myself on you. I felt God was saying something to me and perhaps to you as well. I would like you to spend several more days praying about this. Let's see if the Lord confirms it.

"Vincent, I would also like to give you some tapes and literature that I have on the whole subject of discipleship. Please study them so you have an idea of what we are talking about. I realize all discipling relationships are not the same, but I believe they are very significant to our development in God. I believe the Lord has personally called me to make disciples, and it is entirely possible that you are a person that I could disciple in his ways. If you still feel this way after listening to these tapes, let's meet together, talk about it, and see what the Lord will do."

"That sounds good, Brother Charles. I'll be glad to do that, and I'll get back to you in the next couple of weeks."

Vincent then listens to the tapes. They describe the nature of disciple-making—how it happens, what the qualifications are, and what is expected in the end.

A couple of weeks later Vincent and I meet.

"Well, Vincent, what did you think about the tapes?"

"I felt they were very scriptural, and they were a word from God to me. I believe that is what the Lord wants in my life, and I would deeply appreciate it if you would give me the time that will be necessary."

"Vincent, I believe God's call on your life is that of a pastor. By no means is this a final evaluation. But I have observed that you have a real concern for people. However, it remains to be seen whether you ought to pursue full-time ministry and quit your job, or whether God's call for you is to be a lay pastor, operating over a sphere of our responsibilities here. Why don't we proceed for about six months and then review the situation. At first, we will spend a few hours a week together, and I will give you some assignments. Perhaps we can also meet for some fellowship or share a meal. Then I would like to take you with me into some ministry situations and let you observe what I do. Does this sound okay?"

"It sounds tremendous, Brother Charles. It would really be a privilege to be inside your life and see how the Lord uses you in the ministry."

"One final thing I need to say, Vincent. And that is that the time we spend together will give us an obligation to one another. But beyond that, we have an obligation to the Lord. I want you to be sure that accepting this responsibility is a commitment to the Lord, that you are willing to carry it out to the very best of your ability, that you will make it a priority, and that if you have any problems with it, you will come straight to me with them. Does that seem good to you?"

"Yes, I do believe it's the will of God, and I will commit myself to follow your leadership to the very best of my ability. And if I have a problem with what is happening, I will come straight to you with it."

"Great. In about six months let's stop and reevaluate everything. If God is continuing to lead, then I will begin to give you a course of action to take in further preparation for the ministry. We will also try to evaluate if the Lord wants you to obtain further formal education."

The above is an example of a conversation that may initiate a discipling relationship. It is by no means the only way. I chose an existing Christian rather than a new convert because there are so many people in our churches in that position. They are Christians who know the Lord and want to follow him, but they have not had the personal attention that would help to bring them to maturity and ministry. I have heard scores of Christians say that they asked for that kind of relationship with a pastor but were turned away.

I hasten to add, discipling does not have to be for pastoral ministry. It can be centered in other ministry training.

Once the commitment is made, the time devoted to the relationship becomes a priority for both people. Whether the commitment is to spend two hours a week together or more, it is important to be faithful to it. Jesus lived with his disciples, and they were very close to him each day.

There are many ways to fulfill a time commitment besides isolating two hours for a private time of conversation. Sometimes a more effective use of time is for the disciple to accompany the leader while he handles responsibilities in a practical area. In this way, the disciple can see how a leader conducts himself. While it may not be possible to have a disciple around all the time, he can be a part of prayer meetings or a larger group that is being trained. Or, he can sit in on certain meetings and see how they are moderated. However, there should be some one-to-one teaching times and dialogue about matters of personal interest.

Another helpful way to form a discipling bond is through recreation. Many times a person can learn more about another person by fishing, golfing, or playing tennis with them rather than in a formal or religious setting.

A leader may also encourage the disciple to spend time working on various assignments in scripture study, working on research projects, or working with other leaders who can provide specific help.

It is important to keep the relationship as practical and normal as possible. Superficiality will only confuse the one being discipled and hinder the Holy Spirit from working in the way that he must work if the discipling process is going to succeed.

It is also important to give approbation to the disciple as he learns, as he manifests right responses, and as he shows good insight.

Jesus asked his disciples, "But who do you say that I am?" Peter answered, "Thou art the Christ, the Son of the living God." Jesus immediately said to him, "Flesh and blood did not reveal this to you, but my Father who is in heaven." This was a tremendous confirmation in the presence of the other disciples. The text indicates that Peter did not handle it very well because a few moments later he pulled Jesus aside to rebuke him. Nevertheless, Jesus felt it important to commend him for his spiritual insight. Such commendation from a teacher is a great encouragement and intensifies the disciple's enthusiasm for learning.

One vital aspect of discipling is delegating responsibility to the disciple as he is able to handle it. It is important to begin with small things and see if he pays attention to details. It is also important that the leader be very specific in the delegation so that the disciple knows exactly what is expected from the start. Then the disciple should have the opportunity to give an account of how the assignment was fulfilled.

The Scripture says, "You were faithful with a few things; I will put you in charge of many things." Every Christian as he is being trained should be given a few things to do. As he accomplishes those few things, he should be given additional responsibilities so he can grow, mature, and become useful in carrying out the purposes of God.

There are times when correction must be given. I like to see if the Holy Spirit will do it first so that I do not have to. A relationship that is constantly corrective deteriorates. But let's suppose that our Vincent here has overreacted in several situations. His emotions clouded his reason and his ability to hear God's voice.

First, it is important for me to remember that I have had that problem—which puts me in a position to be patient and gracious. Next, it helps if I can recall how I was treated, or mistreated, so that I can better approach Vincent. Finally, I need a positive view of the situation so that I can get beyond my own reaction to a proposal that will help Vincent release his gifts in a similar situation in the future.

Now it has become obvious that I must speak to Vincent for his sake and mine. I have prayed and the time is right.

"Vincent, I believe that I should talk with you about your recent conversation with Fred. Do you mind if I give you my perspective?"

We had been told in a prior situation that we only had to inform But' Mae dropped.

I have touched a sensitive subject. Authority will not accomplish much here; it will take the Holy Spirit. I must help Vincent relax and be open, or my word will only compound the problem. He is battling condemnation and is likely to be defensive.

"Vincent, I believe you are overreacting to Fred, and I want to stand with you as you try to get past it. Fred can be blunt, and you tend to be sensitive. But the Lord is using you both to strengthen each other."

Now that I have said it, the ball is in his court. There is no use speaking a long time. His face is a little red, and he needs to talk.

"Charles, I don't know how to take that guy. He just doesn't think about what he says or how it strikes people."

Vincent needs to talk. He has feelings that need to be expressed.

"Fred interrupted me and launched into a whole discourse. It wasn't even on what I was talking about. By the time he finished, I didn't want to talk at all. I don't know if I want to be around him. I know the Lord loves him, but I don't have as much patience as the Lord."

"Okay, Vincent, let's say you are right, that he is just like you say he is—and I'm not saying that he is. He is not the issue. You and I are not the issue, either. The only real issue here is the will of God. How are you going to graduate in the will of God if you don't pass the course? This man loves you. There are plenty of blunt people out there, that you have to deal with, who couldn't care less about our sensitivities. Somehow we must reach them. And you have the gifts to do it."

This may or may not resolve the issue. It may temporarily resolve the issue. I have found that some obstacles are not removed; they are just worn down to nothing.

What is important here is speaking the truth in love, calling the learner up to the divine purpose and perspective, and then giving God time to use the word that is spoken.

It is important to remember that the whole discipling

harsh correction leads to withdrawl

process is designed to bring about change, and that the leader's life is a constant reminder to the disciple that he must change. Change may not be the result of a leader telling his disciple what to do but of the leader's example. Whether change comes through the leader's words, or actions, or in some other way entirely, it will be the result of the Holy Spirit dealing with the disciple and enabling him to change. The leader is an instrument of the Holy Spirit to help the disciple see how and where those changes should be made.

SIXTEEN

Advice and Cautions

THE PENNSYLVANIA DUTCH HAVE A SAYING, "Too soon old, too late smart." Some of what I will write was learned after the fact, but I trust, not too late to be useful for others. I am deeply indebted to those who were willing to help me learn.

—Don't use authority to "jerk" the disciple into position. Lead. A good fisherman can land a large fish on a low test line. Authority is not enough to land a big fish. You have to know how to fish. Helping a person deal with a major difficulty or area of weakness takes more than telling him or her to do it right.

—Don't get your identity from your disciples. Get it from your leaders. Your disciples will flatter you.

—Don't accept everyone who asks to be discipled. Be sure the Lord has sent the person; then he will help you do the job. Later, you won't be subject to doubts about the decision.

—Don't disciple the opposite sex directly. It's too dangerous. Besides, the identity transfer can produce role confusion.

—Don't promise too much. Jesus is the pattern, but should we expect to do as well?

—Don't try to disciple a buddy. Familiarity dulls the ears and ends in failure.

—Don't try to be the Holy Spirit. Teach the disciple to listen to the Spirit. Confirm what you can of what the disciple believes the Lord is saying to him. Encouraging a person in spiritual hearing is one of the greatest opportunities of discipling.

—Don't start without goals. Decide what the ministry and character goals are. Set a future time to review the relationship.

—Don't hold the relationship too tightly. Leave the option to follow with the disciple.

—Don't let all the serving go one way. The teacher and the disciple must serve. One learns to, the other stays in practice.

—Don't ignore bad attitude signs. Attitude is more important than action. An infected attitude portends problems. Procrastination in facing it means bigger problems.

—Don't use too many don'ts. It makes the relationship restrictive rather than releasing.

A word about money: don't become dependent on someone you are training. The person should tithe to the church which pays your salary. Don't borrow from a disciple, and be careful about the gifts you accept. It can ruin your relationship. It can be viewed as abuse of authority.

The teacher should have a positive effect on the disciple in several areas; here are some of them:

1. Attitude. A leader's goal should be to help the disciple maintain an attitude of faith toward the Lord, his calling, and his surroundings.

2. Identity. A leader's desire should be to help the disciple to gain a clear knowledge of his or her identity in Christ and come into a place of confidence without pride.

3. Habits. A leader should help a disciple develop self-discipline, holiness, good health, and a wholesome life style.

4. Relationships. A leader's desire should be to help a disciple to develop strong, loyal relationships. He should also help the disciple develop the ability to edify those around him.

5. Financial Responsibility. A leader should try to help a disciple manage money and become productive and prosperous so that he may have resources to share with others in the kingdom of God as well as with others who are poor and needy.

6. Ethical Behavior. A leader should try to help a disciple to be ethical in his behavior so that he or she is considerate of others and thinks in line with biblical ethics. Biblical ethics are quite different from secular ethics. Secular ethics are self-oriented and situational. Biblical ethics are absolute and self-sacrificing for the purpose of God.

7. Spiritual Power. A leader should work with a disciple to help him know the Bible and become sensitive to the Spirit, not relying on his own skills but on the power of the Holy Spirit. He should help the disciple to be prayerful and ready to manifest any spiritual gift. There should be ministry opportunities.

8. Calling. A leader should help the disciple to discover his or her call from God and be trained to fulfill that call.

The discipling relationship is not static. Hopefully, both the leader and the disciple are growing and maturing. Any possessiveness by the leader stifles this process. As I have said, it is easy for the leader to become possessive of a disciple. He may even use the phrase, "My disciple." The terminology may have a biblical basis, but it is loaded with poor connotations. A disciple belongs to the Lord. A leader only serves as a steward to help a disciple grow and mature in the Lord.

In the long run the disciple may become even more gifted and productive than his teacher. This should not intimidate the teacher but rather cause him to rejoice in the disciple's success and be glad that he has had a part in it.

As the discipling relationship progresses and a leader delegates responsibilities to a disciple, he can look at Jesus' relationship to his disciples to see what things he delegated. Jesus' disciples ushered at the meetings. They handled money and paid tax. They prepared the upper room for Passover. They obtained the donkey for the triumphant parade. They healed the sick and cast out devils. They preached the gospel.

There was a progression from ushering at the meetings to the point of actual preaching and pastoral ministry. The disciples were ready. When Jesus ascended and poured out the Holy Spirit, they stood together and proclaimed the gospel with such power that three thousand people were added to the church in a single day.

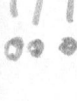

As maturity becomes evident, a disciple needs to be released from the training supervision of the discipler. He needs to be given more responsibility and opportunity to take initiative as circumstances indicate. He must also become more of a friend and less of a student in relating to the leader (though he should always honor the one who led him). The long-term pastoral relationship may continue, but the discipling will come to an end. The more a disciple matures and succeeds, the more he will understand what the leader has done for him, and the more they will be able to sit together as friends. However, the disciple will not fully understand what his teacher has done for him until he disciples someone himself.

Jesus said to his disciples after three and a half years, "No longer do I call you slaves; for the slave does not know what his master is doing; but I have called you friends." The implication there is that the disciples had reached a mature place where Jesus could share with them as friends. It did not mean they were equals with Jesus, but the character of their fellowship was one of friendship and companionship rather than that of a servant to his lord.

At some point it is good to acknowledge to a disciple, "I want you to know things have changed. I no longer view you as a mere student, but I look at you as a friend. I want you to feel free in my presence and let us fellowship and share how God has blessed us together."

A leader must be alert to signs that the disciple is afraid of his teacher. The disciple's intimidation might mean that he is ill at ease around his teacher and unable to communicate his heart. The fear of God is wholesome and healthy. Intimidation, or the fear of man, however, is bad and retards the operation of the love of God.

When the disciple is not progressing properly to maturity, or ministry, it is important to reexamine the original purpose and commitment with the disciple. It may be helpful to have another spiritual person present during the reexamination. Perhaps the method has been wrong, the purpose has been misinterpreted, or other problems have accumulated. All of those areas need to be addressed before the relationship continues.

If the relationship goes sour, the teacher should do all that is possible to avoid ending the relationship in bitterness. If it becomes evident that the relationship is not able to progress, the leader should graciously let the disciple go.

Jesus turned to his disciples on one occasion and said, "Do you want to go away also?" God allows us to follow him from a commitment based on our own will, not based on his ability to control us.

Naomi turned to Ruth, her Moabitess daughter-in-law, and said, "Go, return to your mother's house." Finally Ruth said, "Do not urge me to leave you, for where you go, I will go."

Later Elijah turned to Elisha saying, "Stay here." Elisha responded by saying, "As the Lord lives and as you yourself live, I will not leave you." Elijah did not command Elisha to stay, but he gave him the opportunity.

It is important for a leader to give a disciple the opportunity to do whatever is in his heart and to do it with great freedom and graciousness even though the leader may believe it is a mistake. A leader should tell a disciple if he disagrees, but he should not use his view to bind the disciple to a commitment that is not in his heart. That would not be like our Lord.

A different approach must be used if bitterness has already set in. The Scripture says an offended brother is harder to win than a city. It is therefore important to give a disciple some source of appeal. The person who gives the *leader* spiritual oversight or someone who is a peer in terms of pastoral responsibility can be brought in, and the disciple can be invited to state his grievances without fear of reprisal. He should be encouraged to say all that is in his heart and bring any charges even though they might be completely unjust. It is necessary for a disciple to cleanse his heart of suspicion and accusation.

Such sessions are very painful, but if the teacher can hear it without receiving condemnation, he can benefit. It can also prevent the angered disciple from needing to ventilate his feelings elsewhere or becoming vindictive.

Pastors are not only called to minister to their constituents but also to train them to be faithful people who will train others. Truth is a trust. Those who receive it are required to pass it on. The responsibility comes with receiving the gifts of God.

Years ago I was riding in a rather large boat with a seasoned captain. We were going through an intracoastal waterway, and the boat was making a wake about three feet high. The captain suddenly slowed, and I asked him what was wrong. He said, "My wake is getting too big, and I am legally responsible for it. I have to pay for any damage my wave does."

Leaders are also responsible for their wake. Many times we have made bigger waves than we realized. While we intended no damage, the influence did do damage, and we bear responsibility for it. As pastors, we have a great deal of influence. Let's be careful how we use it.

Part VI:
Care Groups

SEVENTEEN

Why Have Small Groups in the Church?

MANY CHURCHES HAVE SMALL GROUPS. But not all churches with small groups have answered the question whether they are related to the overall purpose of the church. Are they helping the members move ahead as a body of Christians? Or are the small groups spontaneous, subsurface rumor mills that pass along whatever gossip is blowing through the church at any given moment?

I have pastored churches with and without structured small groups. Since 1966 I have been an active promoter of small care groups within the church, which I would define as any group of Christians, usually less than twenty-five, that meets regularly in a home for mutual care, edification, and outreach.

My original reason for establishing care groups in the local church I pastored was that I saw them in the Bible. What I saw in the Bible was what I wanted to see in the church I pastored. The first gatherings of Christians apparently took place in homes (see Acts 2:46; 12:12; Rom 16:5; 1 Cor 16:19; Col 4:15; Phlm 2).

My childhood experiences in small groups along the bayous of south Louisiana also influenced me. And it was part of my nature to seek close relationships with an intimate group of people.

In addition, I had studied enough church history to know that some current denominations and religious movements began as small Bible studies in homes. A good example of this was John Wesley's "classes."

Shortly after my attempt to start small groups, I became aware of others who were doing the same thing. I heard numerous testimonies from pastors experimenting with small subgroups in their local churches. I came across a tract from Bethany Fellowship of Minnesota entitled, "The Last Secret of the Early Church," which advocated small groups.

There are many reasons that care groups should exist in every church. The overriding goal is that the individual Christian can mature and become productive, bringing others into the faith. Care groups are a structure that helps extend the care of Christ to all the members of the church. They involve many people beside the ordained pastor in extending Christ's care.

Here are some purposes of care groups in a large or growing church:

1. To communicate the church's total life and goals to smaller, intimate segments of the church. Small groups help keep everyone involved in the church's life and purpose.

2. To provide teaching of Bible truths under the oversight of the church leadership. In other words, small groups enable us to imitate what was done in Acts 2—to teach the church the apostles' doctrine from house to house.

3. To get more people involved in leadership of the church by training them to lead and care for the small groups. Thus more people are sharing the pastoral burden for all church members.

4. To provide for corporate intercession for church and nation.

5. To provide for corporate edification through the exercise of spiritual gifts.

6. To provide for corporate evangelism. In a small group friends and neighbors can be brought into a personal setting with Christians who are seeking to live out the gospel.

7. To provide for sharing of testimonies and reports of God's work. Sharing in a small group helps to teach people how to share their testimony among non-Christians.

8. To provide for Christians' learning to serve one another in practical ways, helping each other as neighbors.

9. To provide a place for individuals to share their burdens, rather than having them shared throughout the whole church.

10. To support family life. Care groups can offer support by bringing the entire family together into worship with other families who face the same challenges.

11. To bring single people and families into contact with one another. They can share their mutual needs and aspirations with one another in this type of setting.

12. To allow the church to grow to great size while preserving personal care and a sense of belonging. The church will never get too large if there are properly functioning care groups. There will always be an opportunity for close personal relationships even in a very large church.

There are Christians who can develop and become productive without care groups, but many will not. In most evangelical circles, a large percentage of new converts are lost in the first year after their conversion. There is also a very high percentage of inactive members in most all churches. Many of these people are lost to the church because the church did not manifest ongoing love and care for them. After conversion some problem or disappointment seemed to rob the new believer of the promise of faith in God. Having care groups is one way of retaining the resources God gives to the church and preventing wolves from devouring the flock of God.

EIGHTEEN

Making Care Groups Work

CELL GROUPS, GROWTH GROUPS, HOME GROUPS, CARE GROUPS—the name chosen for the small groups established in the church should suggest the purpose that they are to fulfill. The church leadership should give careful consideration to the naming of small groups. Whatever the name, it offers a mission statement for the small group leader and the constituency.

Care groups, as I have sketched them, should operate under church government. They are not the result of initiative from members of the church. Their formation should stem from the leadership's response to the Holy Spirit for the purpose of building up the entire church. Of course, suggestions from the membership may be one way the Lord guides them. If the care groups are formed by the corporate counsel of the church's leadership, they will be responsible to the church leaders and will not become isolated.

Care groups must function under qualified leaders who are approved by the church's leadership. These should be leaders who carry a pastoral concern for their constituents and have more than an ability to lead meetings.

Care groups should meet regularly at a time established by the church leadership. Some churches may find it desirable for them to meet weekly, every other week, or once a month. This depends on the needs of the church and the people involved. Our care groups in Gulf Coast Covenant Church meet every two weeks. This enables the members to maintain close relationships, yet gives them time for other outreach and activities.

Care groups need more than a meeting mentality. They also need a relational mentality. The constituents need to understand that they are related to the leader and one another on an ongoing basis, not just when they are at a meeting. This mentality will encourage them to exercise real continuing care for one another. The members of one's care group are an excellent place to start practicing our covenant love in Christ.

The leader is the most important person in the successful operation of a care group. It is important that he see himself as a steward over this segment of the church and not the proprietor of the people. A stewardship mentality will cause him to be careful in handling the people of God. It will also encourage his sense of accountability to the Lord and to the leadership of the church.

A care group leader can maintain a steward's outlook more effectively if he has a sense of delegation or ordination from the church leadership. If he has been publicly authorized by the leadership, it is easier for them to call him to accountability.

The leader should convene the meeting at the appointed time and place and not simply when he feels led. He convenes it for the purpose explained to him by the leadership of the church.

The leader should set forth the goals of the group to the constituents. Among those goals may be fellowship, worship, teaching, sharing of gifts and testimonies, prayer ministry for various needs, encouragement, corporate counsel, recreational fellowship, and community outreach.

The leader is responsible to keep the meeting and relationships on course and in the flow of the Holy Spirit. He is also responsible to encourage participation, correct the wrong kind of participation, and bring adjustment where it is needed. He must be able to discern whether this correction should be done in the meeting or in private. If in public, it should be done to encourage participation rather than eliminate it. If in private, the leader must have a sufficient bond of love with the one being corrected so his words will be edifying and properly received.

One of the leader's primary goals should be to get everyone involved as much as possible. He must be careful that his own gifts do not dominate the meeting, intimidating others or making them feel they have nothing to share.

The leader must be careful to interpret the meeting to the uninitiated. When new people are brought into the meeting, the leader should explain to them the purpose and procedure of the meeting and what it is hoped will be accomplished. It is important that the uninitiated come to understand the operation of the Holy Spirit and how spiritual gifts function. The leader should see that there is someone following up with the guest.

Last, but not unimportant, the leader should be sure to close the meeting on time. The closing time should be prearranged. If further ministry or discussion is needed, those who are not involved should be released so they can leave. Meetings that tend to be too long will eventually lose support and begin to disintegrate.

The leader's responsibility does not begin and end with the meeting itself. When needs are expressed that cannot be addressed in the meeting, it is important for the leader to follow them up or get a capable person to do so, dealing with them privately. He should also keep the overall church leadership informed of the needs in his group and the progress made in meeting those needs.

Regular care-group leaders' meetings, in which they share their challenges and successes with one another, can be helpful to each care group leader. Meetings also provide a comprehensive picture of the state of the church to the overall church leadership.

Care groups are usually no better than their leadership. They are also no more effective than the degree of participation within the group, since one of the groups' major purposes is to mature each member. Therefore, the church leadership must assume the responsibility of training these leaders to be effective and helping them set the goals that should be achieved. It is important that the goals of the group go beyond their own satisfaction and sense of fulfillment. There ought to be some purpose for the group that lies beyond the group.

Finally, the church must take the responsibility for the success or failure of care groups. If care groups are going to succeed, there must be a corporate decision and effort on behalf of the church to support them. Their relation to the overall life of the church must be defined. Our church policy is that to become a member of Gulf Coast Covenant Church one must belong to a care group and be related to a pastoral leader.

In my opinion, care group leaders are among the most important people for the success of the church. They are not professionals. They serve because of dedication to the Lord and his people. The pastors and the congregation should make every effort to support and encourage those who take on such a vital responsibility.

If the care groups have a clear, positive purpose, good leaders, good participation, and reach new people, they will be a great success and worth all the effort.

But while care groups hold much promise for church life, they also offer some pitfalls. Care groups are certainly not a panacea, and they may not function as intended. Therefore, here are some cautions in the establishment of care groups:

1. Train the care group leadership. Make sure they have the ability to lead and have a strong sense of stewardship under the oversight of the church leadership.

2. Be watchful for a lack of relationship between the overall church leadership and the care group leader. That relationship is a vital connection to the church as a whole. A breach isolates the entire care group, making it vulnerable to problems. It may result in domination and control. An ambitious care-group leader who is isolated from the overall leadership of the church loses the sense of stewardship. The leader becomes the "proprietor" of the group. His teaching is likely to become distorted and produce aberrations among his constituents.

3. Be sure the care groups have a strong sense of purpose. The leadership and constituents should know why they are together. The purpose needs to be spelled out by the leadership of the church. A loss of a sense of purpose will result in stagnation and disintegration.

4. Resist the temptation to become a miniature Sunday morning meeting. While the care group leader should exercise some pastoral ministry, another formal meeting is not what the people need—nor are the ingredients available to perform that type of ministry.

5. Be watchful for lack of variety in the meetings and ministries. Members will not be helped to grow to maturity unless there is a wide variety of spiritual gifts. Without variety, there is the possibility that boredom or overdevelopment may occur in one area, to the neglect of others.

6. Build care groups that are neither too big nor too small. The leadership of the church should discuss the size desirable to suit its needs. Less than twelve adults may not provide the variety of gifts and personalities needed for the group. It may also be too small for the kind of worship and praise that can edify the group. When a group gets larger than twenty or twenty-five adults, it loses the intimacy it needs for people to be able to share freely and remain in an informal setting. The above figures may vary according to the desires of the leadership and the needs of the constituents. But some standardization of group size in the church is desirable from the outset so that groups do not languish for lack of constituents or become so large that they become a dominant force in the church, out of proportion to their purpose.

7. Be watchful for the development of neighborhood problems. This is a practical area for concern. Many people live in urban and suburban settings where parking is limited and noise is undesirable. In recent years there have been several legal challenges to church groups meeting in homes, on the basis of zoning regulations. Therefore, some practical rules should be considered in the development of care groups which would enable people to avoid becoming a nuisance and provoking complaints. Legal questions aside, neighborhood disturbances militate against one of the primary purposes of care groups, that is, to represent the church to the community in a neighborhood setting.

Observing these cautions will enable care groups to successfully fulfill their purpose.

Any living structure must maintain flexibility. Trouble may not mean that the idea is bad; it may mean that there is a change indicated. Sometimes individuals need to change groups, or a leader should step down. As groups grow, they will need to divide.

We are not told how the Jerusalem church dealt with changes in their house groups; we are just told that there were such groups. That is why we need the Holy Spirit. There are no textbooks or charts that are substitutes for the Holy Spirit. The same Spirit that hovered over the earth in creation is hovering over the church. If we will allow him, he will lead us.

Part VII:
Goals of Pastoral Ministry

NINETEEN

Determining Our Direction

HOUSTON MILES, A PASTOR FRIEND, defined a fanatic as: "a person who redoubles his efforts when he loses his sense of direction." Pastors are to be people of purpose, not fanatics. The answer for most pastors' problems is not more effort. What most of us need is a clear sense of direction. I once heard Billy Graham say, "If you aim at nothing, you will hit it."

I believe in setting goals. Every sermon ought to have a clear purpose that is driven home with each point. Every meeting ought to have a purpose, and every structure in the church ought to have a purpose. Any meeting or unit which is not achieving its purpose should either be adjusted or eliminated, or it will become detrimental.

Reviewing the years since I began pastoring, I can see words from God that became mission statements. It has become my practice to periodically give overview messages to the church, which include the words that have come in various years. The year 1957 was my first year in pastoral ministry. The word from the Lord to me was Philippians 3:13: "Forgetting what lies behind and straining forward." In 1964 the word was from Matthew 3:11: "Holy Spirit." It was a milestone word. For the next several years I made the Holy Spirit the focal point of my prayer, Bible study, and preaching.

In 1972 and 1973, the word was "the kingdom of God." It came from the Lord's pattern of prayer, "Thy kingdom come." In 1976, the word was "family." It came as a group of elders met, prayed, and sought God for a model that described our relationships. We felt that God had shown us we were to function as brothers and sisters in Christ.

In 1984, the Lord gave me three key words: reaffirmation, reconciliation, and reaching out. God called me to reaffirm and establish the people in the church in what he had already said to us. He called me to preach reconciliation and seek ways to be reconciled with other Christians, followed by an emphasis on evangelism. The three words became my mission statement for the mid-1980s.

Our local church has approximately twenty members on its full-time pastoral team. We meet for three-day retreats twice annually to review our progress and set goals. The goals have to do with internal structure, growth, and impact beyond ourselves. These days together are vital times to our overall church life.

The pastoral challenge is to translate the heavenly vision into earthly reality. The heavenly vision is the unveiling of a measure of God's eternal purpose. God himself is goal oriented. Ephesians 1:11 says that God calls us to purpose and works all things according to the counsel of his will. God has an objective and he manages by objective.

Wandering is a curse. When God sentenced Cain for killing Abel, he sentenced him to wander. When God sentenced Israel for refusing to enter Canaan, he sentenced the people to wander. A person or group wanders when they no longer have purpose but continue in motion. It is covering the same ground over and over. Without a progressing revelation of purpose, people become undisciplined and destroy themselves.

On the other hand, when God chooses to favor a person or people, he reveals his will to them and calls them to co-labor with him for his eternal purpose. His resources become available to them, and their level of life is greatly increased.

Every great leader has a sense of purpose and destiny. His call is to that purpose. Abraham was not just called out of Ur; he was called to seek a city whose builder and maker was God. Moses was called to bring Israel not only out of Egypt but into the promised land. David was called to defeat Israel's enemies. Jesus was called by the Father to the incarnation, in order to deliver humanity from the oppression of sin and to build a church which would overcome hell. Paul was called by Jesus Christ to preach the gospel to gentiles and their rulers and to unveil the mystery of the church.

The notion that a person is called simply to be a professional in the life of the church does not exist in Scripture. The biblical call is not to profession but to *purpose*.

No person can walk in another's call. Jesus' purpose was unique. It directed his entire life. Hebrews 12:2 says that he endured the cross for the joy that was set before him. His unique redemptive purpose was a joy that kept him on course, even at the cross. When he cried, "It is finished," he was declaring its accomplishment. While we may all have a "cross," a share in his sufferings, on his cross Jesus achieved his goal uniquely and completely.

Only people who know their calling and purpose can say whether they achieve it or not. The apostle Paul said, "I have finished my course and have kept the faith." Such a statement would have been meaningless unless he knew what his course was.

A major task of leaders is to give their people a sense of purpose. People are happiest and healthiest when living for a purpose beyond themselves. The New Testament Christians had a cause—to disciple nations. The mission was so real that many of them sacrificed their lives for it. Not only did they "love not their lives unto death," but they often met death rejoicing and praising God.

The purposeful, sacrificing church of early centuries is somewhat different from the church of contemporary Western culture with its purposeless, self-centered, and stagnant Christians.

Thomas Oden deals with this in his book, *Agenda for Theology*. He traces his own steps as a young minister who lacked an agenda. He describes how he and other ministers followed a social agenda prepared by secular leaders because the theological world seemed to lack its own agenda. The church, he concluded, needs an agenda of its own.

Thus a major requirement of pastors is to know what they are called to accomplish and to communicate that call clearly to their constituents. The mission must be so related to the eternal purpose of God that it will draw the people, their resources, and their very lives to fulfill the will of God in the earth.

Here are some questions which can help us to evaluate the goals we consider setting for ourselves and our constituents.

—Have we heard from God? Is there a revealed mandate for our goal from the Bible and the Holy Spirit?

—Does this goal serve the long-term corporate good of the church?

—Does this goal serve a value above our own self-interest?

—Is this goal concrete or vague? Is there a way to measure progress toward it?

—Is the goal "ours" to the extent that we will accept responsibility for pursuing it? If it does not work out in the time expected, will we blame someone else?

—Is the goal worthy of becoming our priority? Does it inspire us to sacrifice other pursuits?

—Will we develop a strategy, locate the resources, and commit ourselves to the pursuit of this goal?

—Are we willing to communicate this goal to others and solicit their involvement and commitment?

These are but a few of the relevant questions to ask in determining what the will of God is. If the answer to all of these questions is yes, the group is on the right track.

I would suggest that the church leadership set aside several days to discuss these issues and set clear spiritual and practical goals for the church. I would suggest that those goals be presented to the church and that the church be given the responsibility to examine and commit itself to follow the leadership in the pursuit of purpose.

Several years ago, I and the board of directors for *New Wine* magazine asked a consultant, Bill Hautt, to give us advice about the magazine. Bill was an outsider, unfamiliar with our work, but gifted and objective. He interviewed readers across the country, talked with major contributors, interviewed staff people, and finally sat down and talked with me. His first question was, "Why are you doing this?" It took me too long to answer. I realized I had to be able to answer that vital question more directly if we were going to achieve the will of God.

That question motivated me and the staff to spend many hours searching in prayer and consultation. After a year Bill helped us to come to this simple purpose for our publications ministry: "Challenging Christians to live on the leading edge of God's purpose." This became a target for editors, authors, production staff, the art department, marketing people and everyone associated with that ministry.

The church needs the same sort of exercise.

TWENTY

People Goals

DEREK PRINCE HAS SAID in my presence on several occasions, "It takes New Testament people to build New Testament churches." How true. People are the building blocks of the church, and churches will be no better than the quality of the living stone used to build them.

When I began pastoring, my goals were institutional—build a better and larger church. After six years, I began to discover a flaw in my objective; it was people. The church got more people, and in many ways it got better, but we were not converting our converts to a biblical level of commitment and quality of life. We were not producing enough people who were committed citizens of God's kingdom.

Our ratio of members to new converts was about ten to one. We had one baptism for every ten members. Some would put it this way, "It took ten existing members to reach one new Christian." The truth was that one member reached several new converts and the other nine reached none. We had many nonproductive Christians.

In addition, we had many Christians whose lives exhibited little or no real commitment to a purpose beyond themselves. Thirty to forty percent of the membership was relatively inactive. They did not attend or tithe. Many, in fact, were completely out of the church but still on the roll.

One very sobering reality was that our youth were pulled

more strongly toward secular fads than toward spiritual commitment. The dress, music, vocabulary, and attitudes of secular society made strong inroads among them. I saw the condition of the youth as a vital sign of church health.

In sum, I discovered that I could build a larger church and still fail to obtain the basic biblical qualities in the individual members. I realized I would have to rethink my pastoral goals and communicate them on a more personal basis.

Sure there were some very fine people in the church. There seemed to be no really serious problems. Comparing ourselves to other churches might have brought some comfort. But I kept looking in the word of God and at the New Testament church. There I found little comfort for our condition. I looked at the growing influence of secular culture; I found no comfort there.

All of this caused me to look at my own life and the quality that I had to offer. I came under deep conviction of the Holy Spirit in areas such as prayer, commitment, and spirituality. My preaching, I saw, had been "beating the sheep instead of feeding the sheep." I began to feel like singing the old spiritual, "It's not my brother or my sister but it's me, O Lord, standing in the need of prayer." I believe that the Lord spoke in this way, "Charles, you have been at this church six years. If you had more to give them, you would have done so. They are the mirror of your ministry."

The Holy Spirit made my life the issue. I was the pastor, the messenger, the example. If I wanted to pastor a church like I saw in the New Testament, I had to become a man of God like I saw in the New Testament.

I began to seek God in order to be able to impart his life and purpose to the average individual in the church. I began to fast and pray and immerse myself in the word of God. As I have already described, the power of God came into my life in a new dimension and began to equip me to equip the people.

Whatever character or ministry goals we set for the people, the leadership must embody those goals. We cannot impart what we do not possess. Only good trees bring forth good fruit. Wheat produces wheat; apples produce apples.

Nervous pastors cannot produce peaceful people. Take Reverend Flinch, for instance. He needs peace; the Lord gives him some verses on peace for his own need. He appreciates them so much that he prepares a sermon on peace for the people. But he is still nervous.

He begins his message with tentativeness and anxiety. "Fr...friends, I have, what I hope could be a me...message, that will (twitch, scratch) uh...bring peace to your, uh, heart." Red welts are breaking out on his face.

After a few minutes of this, the congregation is breaking out too, scratching, twitching, coughing, and coming down with severe anxiety. "Great, uh, ser...sermon on, uh (scratch, twitch), peace, Reverend."

If you have measles, you can talk mumps, but they get measles. Watch for the little red bumps.

We do not impart what we say. We impart what we are. Our primary goal must be to become what we want the individual Christian to become. The people are expecting and needing an impartation of Christ.

Jesus began his public ministry with the Sermon on the Mount. The Sermon on the Mount focuses on the kind of people that would find favor in the kingdom of God. The Sermon on the Mount demonstrates that God begins with character goals for his disciples. Then he goes on to ministry goals. Christ exalted qualities such as humility, penitence, meekness, spiritual hunger, mercy, purity of heart, and peacemaking. He avoided selecting as disciples those whose primary motivation was to be seen or who judged others by appearance.

In the light of Jesus' own example, what kind of character goals should we establish for ourselves and the individual members of the church? Here are twelve vital qualities in addition to some of those already mentioned:

1. **Humility.** Lowliness of mind. The ability to trust the

Lord to place us in the position he has for us without arrogance or wrong ambition.

2. Love. The divine quality that enables us to personally sacrifice for the good of others.

3. Faith. The ability to have unshakable confidence in something God has said though it has not yet come to pass.

4. Righteousness. Right relationship to God through Jesus Christ and right relationship to those around us. Being right by the grace of God.

5. Worshipfulness. The adoration and exaltation of Christ through gifts, honor, praise, prayer, and physical demonstrations such as clapping and lifting hands.

6. Graciousness. An attitude that delights in blessing God and people. It is demonstrated in hospitality and generosity.

7. Prayerfulness. A relationship with God that produces an awareness of his constant presence, a dialogue with God in the Holy Spirit, and a deferral to his will. It is the quality that disciplines the individual to turn aside for times of giving God full attention.

8. Power. The dynamic of the Holy Spirit operating through the life of the individual Christian to perform any service which God may want to accomplish.

9. Serving. The natural consequence of divine love and grace which compels us to assist each other in practical ways.

10. Honoring. The manifest esteem that Christians have for God and those he esteems—parents, the aged, rulers, leaders, teachers of the word and doctrine, and all of those that honor God.

11. Reconciliation. The ability to communicate the love of God to those who are estranged in or out of the church. This of course includes evangelism.

12. Restfulness. The ability to live in a state of trust and therefore peace.

These attributes are Christ-like. They are indicators of spiritual maturity. I do not find that I produce these personal qualities by striving for them; but by giving attention to the

Lord and his word they are sown in me by the Holy Spirit. As I produce and preach these qualities, they are sown in those who are influenced by my ministry. As they grow up in individuals and therefore the church, they become a firm foundation for great ministry and achievement. They produce an atmosphere that is heaven-like.

It is important for pastoral leaders to remember that they will live with the character foundations they lay. I was privileged along with several other church leaders to visit with a cardinal in a Roman Catholic church in Europe. The tower of his cathedral stood above the rest of the city skyline. It had taken three hundred years to build. One generation after another had built on the work of their fathers and grandfathers. Successive generations of stone masons had built for permanence and stability, knowing that their descendants would work and worship there. As I looked at the tower, I thought about craftsmanship in the body of Christ. Great churches are not thrown together. They are more than spiritual rock piles. They are built of living stones properly related to the cornerstone and each other.

TWENTY-ONE

Church Goals

BY THE TIME I WAS EIGHTEEN YEARS OLD, I knew that I was called to preach. But beyond that I had very little idea of what I would try to accomplish as a man of God. I never sat down and set goals, nor did I hear the voice of God say, "Charles, this is the kind of church you are to build." I instinctively began to work on the Bible-oriented model of my father's ministry. It did not occur to me that there were some basic issues of church life that would have to be resolved.

It would be fair to say that I was a fundamentalist, in the sense that I believed the basic tenets of Bible doctrine as expounded by conservative evangelicals. My Southern Baptist background gave me many blessings. One was the conviction that the Bible was God's word and my standard for faith and practice. Whatever my doctrine and practice would be, it would have to be from the Bible. Without a doubt, I was more than a little naive about the teachings of the Bible and perhaps arrogant about the degree to which I had attained to biblical truth. But I thank God for a basic commitment to Holy Scripture.

From the outset of my ministry, being biblical was the presupposition of all of my preaching and practice. Being biblical, however, is more than owning a Bible. It is also more than proclaiming that the Bible is inspired or that it is our standard, although for several years, my approach was simply that. But being biblical has to do with responding to the God of the Bible, in the same manner as the people in the Bible, and achieving the results produced in the Bible.

On one occasion, I was angered by a seminary professor who said, "You fundamentalists go around with the Bible under your arm. One day it's going to explode and blow your arm off." Sure enough, my Bible exploded. I had greatly underestimated the power of the truth and the Spirit that the Holy Word bears witness to. Nevertheless, it was my commitment to the word that caused me to be willing to change my attitude and methods. And that same commitment held me firmly and guided me through change.

It was in 1963 that I began to see the distinct differences between what I was producing and the pattern advocated by the apostles. I saw the evangelistic lack, the giving lack, and especially the prayer lack in the church. My initial response was to put the responsibility for the lack on the church. But the Holy Spirit would have none of it. He put it on me. He made it clear that the church reflected my own lack. So I began to pray and repent.

In April 1964 when I was filled with the Holy Spirit, the results in my life and in the church were dramatic. Personally and as a church we began to see the New Testament goals for church life more clearly. We also began to move toward them in a more powerful way.

The first goal we made progress toward was **prayerfulness.** Suddenly prayer became a relationship with the Lord instead of a duty. I began to practice the presence of God, aware of and deferring to him more frequently. The Holy Spirit led me to study the prayer life of Jesus. His walk with the Father was a continual dialogue that determined his every move and message. Out of that relationship flowed the supernatural and revolutionary results.

The whole church that I pastored was affected. The Wednesday night prayer service increased in attendance. The ladies wanted a Thursday morning prayer and Bible study. The men wanted a Friday night meeting. The ladies who could not attend on Thursday morning started a meeting on Tuesday night. The church was open all day Saturday until late evening for prayer. Prayer became a priority. We were building a praying church.

During one season men gathered each night for about twelve weeks. We found ourselves compelled by the Holy Spirit to seek the Lord and his power. We were in a school of the Spirit through prayer.

Unusual things happened by God's sovereign direction. On one occasion a lady came for counseling. I had begun to counsel less and pray with people more. As the lady came into my office, the Holy Spirit came on her. Before I could say anything, she fell on her knees and began to pray. Soon she was confessing her need of Christ, repenting, being converted and filled with the Holy Spirit—all without my assistance.

As the years passed, I have seen the prayer rise and subside, but today there is a prayer revival in many churches. The great churches of the world are those that have rediscovered the taproot of spiritual power. The way to recapture the dynamics of New Testament church life is through prayer. Any effort to develop the church while ignoring prayer is an effort to bypass the executive of the church—the Holy Spirit. In contrast, any effort to discover the will of God and acknowledge the Holy Spirit through prayer is a step toward biblical church life.

Prayer and seeking God led me to an experience of the **power of God.** John Wimber calls it a "power encounter." It's difficult to say which comes first, the sense of the purity and holiness of God or the sense of his sovereign power. In my case, we were overcome by his holy power.

The manifestation of the Spirit mentioned throughout the Bible became a reality in my life. Praying in the Spirit or "in tongues" was a daily reality. My devotional life began to affect my whole life. Soon I was sensing a flow of God's direction and power. Sometimes I felt that God prepared me, then urged me to move in spiritual power. While I wanted his power, I had to wrestle with my opinions and methods and with current public opinion.

One day the phone rang. "Brother Charles?" It was Harold, a new member recently baptized. He was a tall man of simple background who had a great tenacity with any truth that he felt came from God. Harold had developed back trouble and had to sleep on the floor. The doctor told him that he needed one and maybe two operations on his back.

"Do you believe the Bible?" he asked.

"Of course I do, Harold. You know that," I responded.

"Well, do you believe James 5:13 and 14?"

"Yes, of course I do. What does it say?"

"It says, if any one is sick, call for the elders. I guess you are my elder. And it says that they should anoint him with oil, and the prayers of faith will save the sick. I've got bad back trouble. I can't work, and I've got to have surgery that I can't afford. I want you to bring your oil and come pray for me."

I felt like I had been had. I was not a "faith healer." I was just a Baptist pastor who wanted the power of God. But Harold challenged me to practice the Bible and reveal the power of God in a needy situation. I loved Harold, but I was unprepared for the faith test.

I will never forget browsing through the drugstore to purchase some sort of oil with which to anoint Harold. "What if someone I know asks me what I'm looking for and why I want it?" I wondered. I settled on olive oil. Had I been asked why I was buying it, I probably would have drunk it on the spot. I paid for it and left the store.

When I arrived at Harold's, he was stretched out on the floor of his bedroom in pain—wall to wall Harold.

"How are you, Harold?"

"Not so good, Brother Charles."

We talked small talk. I did not know how to get down to business.

"Will you anoint me and pray for me, Brother Charles?"

"Yes, Harold." I did not know how to anoint. No one ever

taught me. I touched my finger to the bottle, touched Harold on the head, and prayed. "Lord, if it be your will . . ." I stumbled along tentatively, "Help Harold feel better...uh..." I finally quit, looked at Harold, and felt like a fish out of water.

"Well, Harold, I guess I'll be going now."

"Okay, Brother Charles."

As I left, I felt awful. Harold did not seem any better.

The next morning the phone rang. It was Harold again. "Brother Charles, bring your oil and come back and pray for me. I'm no better."

I thought, "Lord, you are going to have to heal Harold. I know Harold. He will have me over every day from now on if you don't do something." Before I went, I read numerous Scriptures on healing and became assured that God *did* want to heal Harold.

I walked in, poured oil on my hand, slapped it on Harold's forehead: "In the name of Jesus, be healed!" Just like Oral Roberts.

Harold jumped to his feet.

"Praise God! I feel better!"

"Me too, Harold, me too!"

Now I was in the healing business!

The church began to accept the ministry gifts of the Holy Spirit. Of course, some people left, unwilling to change or acknowledge that the power of God was for our generation and our church. But others came because their needs were met. Evil spirits were cast out, financial needs were met, and relationships were healed, all by the power of God.

"I will build my church," Jesus said, "And all the gates of hell will not prevail against it." Jesus' church was a powerful church. Our church was becoming part of *his* church.

Another goal that came into focus was **triumphant church life.** I had always been interested in eschatology—end-time events. I was, without a doubt, pretribulation, premillenial, second coming oriented. But what is more, I maintained an apocalyptic attitude toward society and a negative view of the church's future until after the second coming. I saw no hope for a world-wide revival or a triumphant church.

After I was filled with the Holy Spirit, I experienced a strange phenomenon. When I prophesied under the Holy Spirit, the words were edifying, encouraging, speaking of a triumphant church. But when I preached my eschatology of doom and judgment, the Holy Spirit seemed to depart. Was God not pleased? I became so frustrated that I had to completely lay aside my search to understand end-time events. This lasted for several years. Instead, I found myself preoccupied with resurrection power and a church like I saw in the New Testament—one that prevailed. While I never lost my enthusiasm for the coming of Christ, I came to see that he wanted to return for a different kind of church than the one I had formerly seen.

My faith for the church was rising—and so was the church! The church I saw was the one Jesus died and rose to produce; it was the one he headed from the throne of power; it was the one he interceded for continually; it was the one that Satan feared and fought viciously; it was the one that sinners needed to help them prevail; it was one our people were happy to be a part of. At last, we believed we could experience the triumph of Christ in this world.

The experience of God's power and triumph led on to another goal. We were forced to confront the challenge to become a **caring church**. The supernatural is a most exciting dimension. It attracts all kinds of people. Many of them have serious needs. Our initial joy at God's power at work in them was followed by a realization that many practical answers must come through the love of Christ, the church, and its leaders.

It is the Holy Spirit that heals, but the church is often his instrument. The Lord provides, and the church is often the means that he uses. As needy people came, my work load was greatly increased and again we were driven to the Scripture. Soon I appointed lay pastors and group leaders to share the burden of pastoral care. But beyond that, the entire church was challenged to become Christ's body to care.

Every church or movement that receives the power of God is faced with the challenge to care for those that are drawn to it. Those who are able to continue to care through a divinely appointed structure—without losing the priority of reaching out—will grow indefinitely.

The priority of being **evangelistic**, we came to see, needs to be periodically renewed. In the late 1960s and early 1970s God so impressed us with the need to care that we made it a major priority. Because we did care and showed it in practical ways, many people were drawn to our church and other churches with which I worked. We grew rapidly, without an overtly evangelistic emphasis. But something subtle happened. As I mentioned earlier, we became introspective and inward in our focus.

Care became such a priority that many of our constituents became self-centered. Our evangelistic gifts became rusty. It took several years for this trend to become sufficiently evident to cause us trouble. By the early 1980s we sensed that something was wrong. Those with evangelistic gifts were not challenged and developed, and many of the churches with which I worked had ceased to have significant growth.

In 1983 I took several months off to regain a sense of perspective. The Lord impressed me with the importance of refusing to take on responsibilities that resulted in mere maintenance and were unrelated to mission. He spoke to me about delegating my work and pruning it back. He began to tell me to reach out.

Within a couple of years, there was ample evidence that many of the churches that I worked with were reaching out and evangelistic gifts were beginning to function. The power was also returning and manifestations of the Spirit were multiplying. There was a renewed emphasis on equipping the members of the body to do the work of Christ.

Perhaps in any one season we have to focus on some truths to the exclusion of others. But for us, neglecting the evangelistic emphasis was expensive. Because we failed to challenge them, we lost some whose gifts could have been a blessing. We allowed some to become preoccupied with lesser things. Worst of all we had become habitually unevangelistic in some quarters. And habits do not change quickly.

Evangelism has to be a continual goal. Failing to emphasize the importance of leading people to Christ has the same result that a farmer's failure to plant will have. There will be no harvest. To the extent that a church falters in evangelism, it falters in reproducing a truly New Testament Christianity.

One of the goals we share in our local church is to see every Christian involved in church life in two ways. One, we would like everyone to be a part of a pastoral unit, a care group; two, we want **all the members to be a part of a ministry team** that contributes to some purpose beyond themselves.

In that pursuit, we have established fifteen or more ministry teams. The purposes are to fill a real need in or out of the church and to develop the gifts and ministries of the church. People who are cared for but who do not get into ministry stagnate. Maturity can only come with productivity.

We have teams that serve in areas such as music, youth, prison ministry, buildings and grounds, athletics, business advice, hospitality, and ministry to the poor. Some churches may form committees to deal with these areas. My experience is that committees tend toward analysis instead of action. Teams are people who are spiritually gifted and called to act on these areas. They are led by people who are action oriented. The teams not only function to meet needs and develop members' gifts, but they can serve as evangelistic units to reach out to people in the community who share the same interest.

Church leaderships should consider how to challenge every bona fide gift of God to be used for the glory of God. The possibilities for a variety of ministry teams are numerous.

It is a tremendous goal to have all the members of the body properly related to each other. It is an even greater goal to see them also *functioning* together to achieve the purpose of God.

One of the immediate challenges that faced me in 1964 was that our church had borrowed money to build. Any disturbance and subsequent loss of members would jeopardize our finances. In fact, those who were in opposition to my experience of the Holy Spirit used finances as a threat. I was concerned. I soon saw, however, that the Holy Spirit motivated people to give. Instead of going under, the finances remained strong and grew as the Holy Spirit moved among us.

I had always taught and practiced tithing, but now I was seeing an attitude of graciousness. Isaiah 58, 2 Corinthians 8 and 9, and other passages opened a higher dimension of grace and graciousness to us. Acts 2 and 4 recalled an era in the church when people gave sacrificially to help others spread the gospel.

Giving became more than the release of resources; it became an exercise in sowing seed for future harvest. It became an expression of faith in Christ and his word and his kingdom. It also became an **attitude of generosity** that permeated church life and relationships. The people not only gave to God but to each other.

Giving liberally to the Lord and his work is a most eloquent expression of love and faith. Laying down an offering is in fact laying down life that was spent to earn the money being given. The church that fails to yield to the Holy Spirit in this dimension is withholding the seed that it should sow. The end will be poverty instead of prosperity.

Tithing is not giving. The tithe is a debt that we owe the Lord as owner of creation and king of the kingdom. It is the owner's and ruler's portion. But giving above the tenth is an expression of love and faith that announces to God and society that the giving Christ is among his people.

While we are speaking of goals for local church life, it is important to include **missionary involvement** as a primary goal. The sending out of missionaries and international teams is directly related to all of the previously stated goals—being biblical, prayerful, powerful, triumphant, evangelistic, caring, ministering, and giving. International outreach is the logical, spiritual consequence of each and every one of these goals. That result is amply demonstrated in the Bible and wherever spiritual renewal takes place.

Karl Strader's Carpenter's Home Church of Lakeland, Florida, strives to give 50 percent of its offerings to missions. This goal was set before the church even as they built a ten-thousand-seat auditorium. Ken Sumrall's Liberty Church in Pensacola, Florida, has had a similar goal, even as they have built a large congregation. But this applies not only to churches in the United States. The great churches being built in the Third World are also sending out missionaries.

The church has a world purpose. And that is the subject of the next chapter.

TWENTY-TWO

World Goals

NO CHANGE HAS COME TO MY THINKING with more difficulty than my change in worldview. My mentality toward the world was to see it as evil, something to be escaped. I did not differentiate between the world system and creation itself. I had no hope for nations; Satan was in control. I had never understood the dominion mandate given to Adam, or Christ, over creation. Consequently, I offered my people no world vision beyond "snatching souls from hell."

The more I studied the Bible, the more I saw God the creator's love for creation. I saw creation groaning under the fallen management of unredeemed people. But the Scripture promised a new mankind, justified in Christ, who would be entrusted with the earth. I was facing a new set of questions.

If indeed the entire earth is the Lord's, as Psalms 24:1 says, and if he intends to fill it with his glory, as the Scripture says repeatedly, and if he has delegated to redeemed mankind the task of ruling creation, what is the church's mission to the world?

The local church is not an end in itself. It is the light to the world. The local church has a responsibility for God's goals in the world. Ern Baxter likes to say, "The Lord is a world person." The Bible says, "God so loved the world" and "Go into all the world." That being so, the church must discover God's perspective on the world.

If an entire community should accept Christ, as has often happened in history, how should the church influence the affairs of that community? Any? A lot? Totally? Should city hall be run from the pastor's office? What about business, education, and the military?

Where the church is growing in size and influence, these are not remote questions. The potential impact of a growing church is not lost on today's secularists, atheists, and others who do not want Christian influence.

What does it mean to disciple nations? Should we accept the reality of a pluralistic world? Are Marxism, Islam, and Buddhism realities that we must accept? Does it matter, in fact, what religious philosophy, or lack of it, a nation accepts? These are questions we must answer clearly.

While it must be said that the weapons of our warfare are not carnal, and that flesh and blood are not our real enemies, and that flesh and blood will not inherit the fully revealed kingdom, we are nevertheless faced with the biblical mandate to disciple nations. Are we to take the commission seriously? Are the saints really supposed to judge the earth? Will the kingdoms of this world in fact become the kingdom of Christ?

To back away from these questions, to retreat, accommodate, and escape, is a luxury that we can no longer afford. Our children will live in a world fashioned by others of unholy hands. They will be under extreme pressure either to capitulate or face persecution and death. The responsibility will be ours.

On the other hand, the church may decide to obey its Lord. It may become infused with the power of Christ's resurrection and see what is *his* inheritance in the church. It may opt to pick up its mandate to reign with Christ. It may decide to declare the kingdom of God to all the nations and disciple them in the ways of God.

The church may decide to take its prophetic posture toward civil government and declare the moral values that make people governable and productive. It may shape the kind of people that will ultimately exercise leadership in education, industry, politics, and media.

My purpose here is not to offer specific answers to questions about Christians' role in the world, but to pose the questions. The church must not default in carrying out its biblical mandate in the world. It must decide to face these issues—and act.

There are some practical steps that church leaders can take toward the development of a world strategy within their churches.

—Establish the conviction that the earth is the Lord's and he is sovereign.

—Establish the universality of the church's mission.

—Establish the message of God's present kingdom firmly in the minds of the people.

—Develop a biblical position on moral issues and state it clearly.

—Appoint teams of called and gifted individuals to study the Bible as it relates to civil authority, economics, education, and morality. Consult with historical and contemporary Christian studies that have adopted a biblical posture.

—Encourage these teams to cooperate with other Christian groups that are similarly concerned to express God's ways to civil society. One church cannot do the whole task.

—Use your biblical worldview as an evangelistic tool to win people to Jesus Christ and his ways.

The sequence of eschatological events is God's choice. Every Christian ought to agree that Christ himself is the Omega, the end of all things. In whatever way the events of judgment, deliverance, and a revealed kingdom fall into place, righteousness and wickedness will exist together in this world until Christ's appearing. The point we make here is that the church will be in a triumphant, not retreating, mode. It will be this body that will have been prepared to take the kingdom responsibility when he appears.

The most often quoted Old Testament passage in the New

Testament is Psalm 110:1: "The Lord says to my Lord: 'Sit at my right hand, till I make your enemies your footstool.'" Peter quotes it under the Holy Spirit's power at Pentecost, and Paul declares it in connection with the gospel and resurrection in 1 Corinthians 15:25: "For he must reign until he has put all his enemies under his feet."

The evangelical church is being forced to an agonizing examination of its eschatology by the pressure of other world movements. In my estimation, the Holy Spirit will force an eschatological revolution. Indeed it has already begun. It is not a liberal-conservative issue. It is the practical result of our having left the field to others for so long. The enemies of Christ are not passive, but neither is the Holy Spirit of God. The issues are no longer far off and abstract. They are on the shelves of our neighborhood newsstand, in our child's classroom, in our neighborhood abortion facility, and on our television.

The goal of an aggressive, triumphant church in the world is not as easy to measure as church growth. But if our Lord tarries, our children will tell us if we succeeded.

Part VIII:
Pastors Relate to Other Pastors

I wonder whether the Holy Spirit movement was not given to unite the church. Instead it separated it.

TWENTY-THREE

Standing Together

MY FATHER RESPECTED AND SUPPORTED OTHER PASTORS. He was regularly at the pastors' conference of our denomination and served as the president of the local Baptist pastors' conference more than once. He was a good example of a cooperating pastor. When our pastors' association assisted in building a college, he was right in the middle of the project. When our Baptist churches opposed legalized gambling at the dog track, he led the committee. It always seemed right to me that pastors should stand together.

At age twenty-six, I was elected secretary of our local Southern Baptist pastors' conference. It was a great honor. I was part of a great group of men. It was not long, however, until my relationship with my fellow pastors became strained because of my charismatic renewal experience the following year. The subsequent division was very painful. I was isolated.

The charismatic dimension exposed me to an undefined world of amazing variety. Soon I was fellowshipping with charismatic renewal Baptists like Ken Sumrall, Pentecostals, Episcopalians, and Catholics—all at the same time. Just a few years earlier I had been safely in a denominational context where I had been devotedly anti-ecumenical—more so than most of my brethren. But now I needed pastor friends outside the denomination who understood my experience and the new challenges that I faced.

In 1967 I began meeting with James Kofahl, an Assemblies of God pastor who became a real friend. James and I decided to invite Pentecostal evangelist Nicky Cruz to our city, Mobile. A Catholic priest, an Episcopal priest, and others joined us in the venture. The meeting was a great success. I began to discover Christ in my brother pastors from other denominations and groups.

Soon I was traveling and encountering men of God of national prominence from diverse religious backgrounds. I met Kenneth Hagin, Kenneth Copeland, John Osteen, Dr. Kevin Ranaghan—a Catholic theologian—and Steve Clark, and Ralph Martin who were also Catholics. Then I developed a friendship with Larry Christenson, who was Lutheran. We could discuss baptism without straining our relationship. I was amazed at these new ministerial bonds that I was developing.

I ministered with Dennis Bennet, an Episcopalian; Jamie Buckingham, a former Baptist; Derek Prince and Bob Mumford, nondenominationals; and Don Basham, a Christian Disciple. Then I met "Brick" Bradford, a Presbyterian, and Costa Deir, a Pentecostal missionary. So the list grew. We had some moving demonstrations of unity and love in communion and celebration. In the charismatic renewal we experienced the Spirit of God lifting us beyond our divisions into a joyful event of ecumenical fellowship and cooperation in the church. The theme song seemed to be, "We are one in the Spirit."

In 1970, as I have said, three of these men and I committed ourselves to walk together and submit our ministries to one another because we saw that ministers need one another. We had all seen the truth of Ecclesiastes 4:1-9, "Woe to him who is alone when he falls." Later, Ern Baxter joined us in our desire to find protection and care in committed pastoral relationships.

In the midseventies a number of controversies arose that seemed to virtually destroy the euphoria of unity. In spite of the apparent unity of the 1977 Kansas City charismatic renewal conference, there was deep division among various leaders and their constituents. In the mideighties the tide seemed to begin flowing back toward unity.

The ebb and flow of ministerial unity has existed through the centuries and is a testimony of our carnality. Somehow God endures our pettiness, pours out his Spirit, and draws us together again.

The apostle Peter spoke for many of us when he so zealously declared to Jesus, "Though all men forsake you, yet I will not!" However, a few days later, he swore that he never knew the Lord. Then he went out and wept bitterly.

Sometimes we have to sing our choruses of dedication and then go out to discover that we were not where we thought we were. The chorus was right, but we were not really there yet.

The amazing thing about Peter was that in a few days he had been restored to the Lord and given a new degree of responsibility for the church. And Acts 2:14 makes this statement: "But, Peter, standing with the eleven..." Peter was standing with his brothers at Pentecost, and thousands were converted to Christ as he preached with spiritual power. He became a team player.

It seems that Peter had to experience unusual failure in order to come to the place where he could stand with the brothers. Most pastoral leaders are men of zeal and confidence. It is easy for us to feel like, "I'll do it if no one else does!" Some of us need to experience difficulty and failure before we see the value of having brethren to stand with.

Years ago I heard a story about a young Presbyterian minister who was the visiting minister of a large congregation. Fresh from academic success, he strode confidently into the pulpit. But rather than impressing the congregation, he bombed and he knew it.

After the service he approached an elder. "What went wrong?"

"Well," the elder observed, "if you had walked up like you walked down, you might have walked down like you walked up."

It does seem sometimes that we must experience failure in isolation before we can experience success through working together.

Sometimes we look to the Old Testament for the model of leadership. Moses gives us the image of a great leader aloof from humanity and alone with God. But that approach was too much even for Moses. His Monday morning prayer recorded in Numbers 11:15 was something like this: "Lord, if this is going to be my ministry, kill me, I pray thee."

The Lord's solution for Moses' problem was to have him gather seventy elders to the tabernacle so that they could receive the Spirit and bear the load with him. They did gather and the seventy were filled with the Spirit and prophesied. This became a Hebrew precedent for leaders standing together. Pentecost, hundreds of years later, was in that tradition.

Many people have attempted to make the isolated prophet of the Old Testament a pattern for the church. However, it was not even the universal or normal pattern in the Old Testament. Prophets were isolated because they were rejected. Whenever the people of God are functioning normally, the ministries are not isolated from the body. Even in the Old Testament, prophets gathered others around them and established schools and companies of prophets that worked together.

Acts 13 gives an illustration of leaders standing together to hear the message of the Spirit and to send out Paul and Barnabas. Acts 20 records Paul's address to the gathering of the Ephesian elders. The biblical pattern is that pastors, elders, bishops, whatever their description, function together. In so doing not only are *they* protected but so are their constituents. Plural pastoral leadership insures that the people of God have a more balanced view of God's word, a greater variety of spiritual gifts, and protection against false leaders.

Pastoral fellowship and cooperation, when it is thought of at all, is usually considered within a particular denominational context. But it has great value when it involves leaders joining together from across denominational divisions. Even while we respect our differences, we can love each other and learn to work together. Cooperation does not mean co-equality. There are those who will emerge to lead any group, even a leadership group. Neither the Lord nor the people will allow a leadership vacuum. Just as Peter spoke up at Pentecost and Paul led ministry to the gentiles, leaders will emerge. But no leader should stand alone as a way of life and ministry. The church is a body, and this is meant to be reflected in the leaders.

The success of the early church cannot be divorced from the success of its leaders in working together. Restoration of New Testament church life will require healing in pastoral relationships. This healing will enable pastors to stand together and bring their gifts together for the health of the overall body of Christ. However, discussions of ecclesiology and theology are not the place to begin this process. Rather, it must be started on our knees, in the presence of God, and under the active lordship of Jesus Christ.

Ecclesiastes 4:9-12 declares the wisdom of God regarding relationships. It teaches that two are better than one, and a threefold cord is not easily broken. It also says that a man who is alone when he falls is in great trouble because there is no one there to pick him up again.

James 5:17 clearly states that spiritual leaders have great tests. Being a spiritual leader does not make one exempt from the normal temptations of life. If anything, it heightens them. For this reason pastoral isolation is most dangerous. Without plural leadership, strength, protection, redemption, counsel, and revelation are missing, as when one strand of rope stands alone.

Don Basham records the pitfalls of ministry isolation in his book *Lead Us Not into Temptation*. In his chapter entitled "Why God's Ministers Fall," he describes the tragedy of a successful radio and television minister who, without the protection of a relationship with other leaders, becomes involved in adultery. Then his isolation leads him to reject the loving counsel that fellow ministers offer.

It is clear that Jesus sent his disciples out two by two. He never intended that any disciples be caught alone in a bad situation. Jesus agreed with the warning, "Woe to him that is alone when he falls."

The great tasks of modern life cannot be accomplished alone. There was a day when the isolated craftsman and his wife could farm, make pottery, build a house, and provide for the rest of their family needs. Today, however, it usually takes many people working together to produce the whole result. Modern projects usually require specialized skills and are so large in scale that a large number of people must work together. Each person must do his or her task in order to produce the finished product. It is no different in the church. A pastor can continue as a one-man craftsman doing his little job, but he will be light years behind a society that is moving ahead with expanded thinking and production. The magnitude of a ministry will be determined by the magnitude of the resources. The great churches of our generaton are those which successfully bring many ministries together in a functional way.

While building a great local church is a worthy task, there are even larger issues at hand. The greatest issue is world evangelization, which will require the cooperation of a multitude of leaders.

Competition and duplication not only waste resources but frustrate the Holy Spirit. They are a testimony to human egotism and a reflection of carnality in ministry. Unilateral action and individual attempts to undertake what can only be done by corporate effort are doomed to failure and embarrassment. The ability of the church to rise beyond its past prominence and carry out its mission in the earth today is dependent on the ability of the men and women of God to work together.

A while back I was talking with Kenneth Copeland, whose emphasis over the years has been primarily on faith and prosperity. My own emphasis has been on covenant, discipling, and Christian relationships. We discussed how we had become divided because of a difference in emphasis. Ken made a statement which I will paraphrase. He said, "We would have been better off if we had grouped with each other in our diversity rather than with all those who think the same way." I heartily agreed.

Those who stress covenant would be healthier if they had those among them who stressed faith and prosperity. Likewise, those who stress faith and prosperity would be better off if they had those among them who stressed covenant and relationships. One reason this does not happen is that it is hard for people to be tolerant toward those who say something that is different. Because we cannot acknowledge that these gifts are set among us by the Lord, we suffer in isolation from God's provision. Not only do individuals suffer in isolation from the other gifts, but whole movements suffer.

Variety heals our blindness. Variety adds protection. Variety can add authority to our counsel because there is greater wisdom and greater breadth of the word of God. Variety in our leadership councils will also enable us to oversee a broader group of people, who will therefore hear the counsel and submit to its wisdom.

God has called the church in this generation to touch the entire world with the gospel of the kingdom. In order to do that, pastors must embrace the principle that God has joined us together as leaders in the one body of Christ, even when we do not yet see our unity functioning. We must not compromise our consciences by accepting less than the word of God demands.

Pastors must come to the realization that even when we are able to achieve personal success without cooperation, it will not substitute for church success. Church success will be the result of working together. If the church fails, none of us can rejoice in personal success.

We must be willing to accept our brothers and sisters in leadership and to recognize the diverse gifts among them. We must also be mature enough to recognize those who are anointed to be "helmsmen" and lead the leaders, so that we can move forward together toward the purposes of God.

I do not think that what I am saying about pastoral unity is naive or empty idealism. I have labored many hours in ecumenical settings with strong men of diverse convictions. We cannot ignore the existence of denominations. Unity will not come by being critical of them.

We cannot ignore the fact that some teaching is out of balance or even erroneous. Error must be lovingly and firmly confronted, hopefully with a view to reconciliation.

We cannot ignore the fact that people are hurt by various movements and teachings. They must be helped without picking up their hurt and adding fuel to the bitterness.

We cannot ignore the fact that some leaders cannot share communion together, recognize each other's baptism, or recognize the validity of each other's theology.

In my view, however, the single biggest barrier to pastoral unity, and therefore church unity, is not any of the above. The biggest barrier is the flesh. We are afflicted by the same pettiness and power struggles that afflict our people. If theology and ecclesiology were the main barriers, then denominations would have great internal unity and nondenominational churches would have great internal unity. But as we all know, neither are showcases of unity. The greatest barrier we must overcome is us. God's action in the cross, the resurrection, and Pentecost offers us the way for it to happen.

We must see beyond our present circumstance to God's intention. We must acknowledge Jesus as the head of the church, and the Holy Spirit as his agent on the earth. We must acknowledge the hand of God at work among us all, and what this says about unity among God's people.

Several years ago, I was privileged to accompany a small group of ecumenical ministers to Rome and attend a general papal audience. We were seated in reserved seats up front. During the audience we were asked to stand and were recognized before the nine thousand or more in attendance. It was a very festive and joyful occasion. I marveled at my own journey from a very conservative Southern Baptist background to this auspicious occasion at the Vatican. I turned to one of my pastor friends and smiled.

"Well," I said, "I finally made it to the top—but it's the wrong group!"

God has a sense of humor. There I was, isolated by controversy from many of these who shared my own heritage, enjoying the affections of the Pope and his friends. I was reminded by the Holy Spirit of a day many years earlier when I had been asked to close a local Baptist pastors' conference in prayer. I was only twenty-five or twenty-six years old. I prayed, "Lord, thank you that we don't need a pope." Here I was now, welcomed by those who recognized one.

God has ways of bringing us together. I pray that it will be by divine insight, not sorrowful hindsight.

TWENTY-FOUR

Pastoral Ethics

MANY YEARS AGO, our local Baptist association agreed to set aside one special Sunday to take a census of our county. All of the churches were assigned surrounding areas for census. Each church solicited its people to help, organized teams, and worked in anticipation of the great joint effort to reach out to its prospective members.

One week before the day of the census, a neighboring pastor took a census of the area assigned to our church. He had "jumped our claim." I was only twenty-two years old and not long out of college. I was livid. It not only angered me; it disappointed me that a pastor would be so unethical.

But as the years have passed, I have had greater disappointments. I have watched ministers destroy each others' flocks and reputations. I suppose the greatest of all disappointments is when I have realized that wittingly or not I have also violated the ethic in which I believe. Pastoral ethics are like laws; it is easier to know them than keep them.

Ethics is the science of moral conduct. There are many ethical systems espoused by philosophers and religions. All are not alike. Contemporary secular ethics and biblical ethics are quite different.

The biblical ethic is a covenant ethic. A covenant ethic is a code of conduct shared by a community that has been bound together. The new covenant ethic is one established by the blood of Jesus Christ, by which God has bound himself to the church. Christian ethics are the ethics of Jesus, imparted to the Christian community through the new covenant. When a person accepts Jesus Christ, he also accepts the covenant and the ethic that Jesus established. He also accepts all of those who believe in Jesus. The one loaf and one cup of communion are a demonstration of this covenant. By accepting the covenant, one also accepts all of those with whom the Lord has made covenant and one becomes obligated to serve the corporate interest. It is this covenant which governs one's behavior toward the Lord, oneself, one's family, other Christians, and the unconverted and unredeemed.

The new covenant can be accepted or rejected, but not altered. It is God's covenant. It does not originate with us any more than the Ten Commandments originated with Moses. We cannot alter the stipulations of the new covenant any more than Moses could change what was written in stone.

Ordination is a pointing out and setting in order of ministry. It is also a confirming of a certain authority and gifting. In addition, ordination is an entrustment of the Christian covenant ethic. It is a commission to practice, teach, and maintain the new covenant ethic, and, if necessary, to discipline in line with it.

Christians do not have a personal ethic outside the new covenant. The moment one accepts Jesus Christ, he accepts the covenant ethic. The corporate ethic becomes personal. The moment one becomes a leader in the church, he accepts the responsibility to uphold and propagate the corporate new covenant ethic.

Sin not only violates another individual, but it also violates the covenant and the God who gave it. Therefore, when one sins, he does not simply break a rule, but he breaks the covenant. Thank God for Jesus Christ and his blood that continually cleanses us from all of our sins as we confess and repent of them.

It is the corporate nature of covenant which caused David to declare in Psalm 51, "Against thee, thee only, have I sinned." When David committed adultery and caused Bathsheba's husband to be killed in battle, he not only violated Bathsheba, her husband, and the nation, but he had sinned against God who established the covenant forbidding adultery.

When one attacks a brother or sister, it is an attack on Jesus Christ who has forgiven and redeemed them. It is an attack on his blood which has cleansed and sanctified them. We are not allowed to judge God's elect.

New covenant ethics are not simply stated all together in one Bible chapter headed "Rules." We have to be acquainted with the entire New Testament and open to the action of the Holy Spirit in order to come to grips with the demands of the new covenant. The following are *some* of the ethical requirements of the new covenant. It requires that we

—put God first and worship no other God.

—love our neighbors as ourselves.

—honor our parents and the family as an institution.

—bear one another's burdens.

—bear our own burdens.

—be truthful with one another.

—not accept accusations against one another and, in particular, against leaders without witnesses.

—live morally upright lives (and it declares that violations such as immorality and drunkenness can cost people their place in the kingdom of God).

—put reconciliation and forgiveness before gift giving and offerings.

—break fellowship with one another only as a last resort, and then only if the church has handled the issue in a biblical manner.

—do everything toward the Lord and one another out of the love of God within us.

—cover rather than uncover our brothers' and sisters' problems and weaknesses.

I believe that the New Testament requires all that the Old

Testament does unless explicitly abrogated. However, there are important differences between the two covenants. The old covenant was written in stone, the new in the heart. The old covenant was mediated through the temple system, the new covenant through the blood of Jesus and the power of the Holy Spirit.

The new covenant ethic is nothing if it is not caring. God cared and therefore he took the initiative to reconcile us to himself. If we accept the new covenant ethic, we accept the responsibility to care. Even under the old covenant, each one was his brother's keeper.

Not long ago, a book attacking some very prominent and successful Christian leaders was published and became very popular. The book accused ministers from a wide variety of backgrounds. The author of the book sought to prove that Christianity had been seduced by a false spirit. He quoted and sometimes misquoted those he vilified. These ministries were put in a very bad light, often without sufficient evidence or sound argumentation. The book hurt them, some seriously. I believe that many of the men the author named are genuine servants of God. I have inquired to see if the author of the book had gone to those that he accused before putting his charges into print and, to the best of my knowledge, he did not.

This, of course, is not a new problem. What makes it so sad is that the church has not yet learned to reject so-called correction that is ministered unethically. It is too easy to make public accusations without answering for the irresponsible use of freedom.

Unless a person has ever picked up a book, tape, or magazine article which called their name and misconstrued their heart and message, they do not understand the sadness it causes. Christians, and certainly pastors, cannot indefinitely allow open season on servants of God, without calling for accountability. God will not continue his blessing on these who relish the fall of another.

In 1971 a group of Christian leaders in the charismatic

renewal from many different groups met in Seattle, Washington, to handle some problems which had arisen regarding teachings on water baptism, demonology, and a growing tendency of ministers to attack one another. After much discussion the following statement was written and endorsed by those present. It is one of the finest statements of its kind that I have ever read.

1. We believe that God has set us in positions of leadership within the body of Christ, either as leaders within a local congregation, or as preachers with a ministry to the body of Christ at large, or in a combination of both these ministries.

2. As far as we are able, we will seek at all times to keep our lives and ministries sound in respect of ethics, morals, and doctrine.

3. We will acknowledge and respect all others who have similar ministries and who are willing to make a similar commitment in respect of ethics, morals, and doctrine.

4. If at any time we have any criticism or complaint against any of our brother ministers within the body of Christ, we will seek to take the following steps:

First, we will approach our brother directly and privately and seek to establish the facts.

Second, if thereafter we find grounds for criticism or complaint, we will seek the counsel and cooperation of at least two other ministers, mutually acceptable to our brother and ourself, in order to make any changes needed to rectify the situation.

Finally, if this does not resolve the criticism or complaint, we will seek to bring the whole matter before a larger group of our fellow ministers, or alternatively, before the local congregation to which our brother belongs.

In following these steps, our motive will be to retain the fellowship of our brother and to arrive at a positive, scriptural solution which will maintain the body of Christ.

5. Until we have done everything possible to follow the

steps outlined in paragraph four, we will not publicly voice any criticism or complaint against a fellow minister.

6. In our general conduct toward our fellow ministers and all other believers, we will seek to obey the exhortation of Scripture to "pursue what makes for peace and for mutual upbuilding" (Rom 14:19).

The same statement was reaffirmed by a similar group meeting in Ann Arbor, Michigan, on December 17, 1975.

Christianity is first and foremost a redemptive system which God established through the death, burial, and resurrection of Jesus Christ, his continual intercessory work, and the outpouring of his Spirit. But it is also a system of ethics which is embodied in the life of Christ and in the church. The credibility, and therefore the advance, of the gospel on the earth is directly related to the ethics of the church. Jesus Christ was, and is, a credible savior because he was ethical. He was perfect. Had he not been perfect in all his ways, he would not have been acceptable to God as the sacrifice, and believable by men as the savior of the world. The sinlessness of Jesus and his sacrifice on behalf of others cannot be separated. To do away with one is to do away with the other.

Most of us seem to understand that about Jesus, and yet we often ignore the link between the church's ability to declare the gospel and its ethical posture. The church must not only perpetuate the gospel of Christ, but it must also perpetuate the ethics of Christ. To the extent that we maintain the ethics of the Lord and relate properly to one another, we will be credible in the proclamation of the gospel which brings men and women into the kingdom of God.

There cannot be a dichotomy between ethical character and spiritual power. An ethical character is the foundation for the proclamation of power. And it is an ethical foundation which prevents us from being destroyed when the power of God is displayed. Once we become instruments of God's power, our character becomes the immediate target of public scrutiny and Satan's attack. If he can destroy our character and our ethics, he can destroy our credibility, thus muting the voice of salvation to the world. Today, successful Christian spokesmen are under tremendous pressure concerning their financial and moral behavior. The entire church needs to pray for the leaders that are highly visible.

Christian ethics and spiritual power are the means by which pastors can stand together and succeed in the purpose of God. Practicing new covenant ethics is the only way we can stand together. We must not only see the new covenant as the record of God's actions and teachings but as the mandate for our conduct toward one another. If the church recaptures both the ethic and the power of the gospel, it can recapture what it has previously forfeited—dominion under God.

I do not believe external opposition has the power to defeat the church. No "ism" can overcome the resurrection power of Christ. The single most damaging instrument of the enemy is strife among leaders which debilitates and paralyzes the church. Covenant love slams the door on the enemy. It motivates leaders to stand together for Jesus' sake and reach out to the world for which he gave his life.

Conclusion

WHEN KING SAUL FINALLY DEMONSTRATED that he could not obey God, the Lord told Samuel to stop grieving over Saul and go anoint a new king. The new king, David, would have a heart like God's. David was a shepherd king. He combined the heart of a shepherd and the courage of a warrior.

Later God told the spiritual leaders of Israel that he had rejected them because they did not care for the people. He promised to raise up new shepherds.

Finally Jesus came, and he rebuked the spiritual leaders of his day. He began to select new leaders—less educated, perhaps, but more committed, courageous, and caring.

The Holy Spirit is visiting the church once again, and I believe he is saying these things once again. God is concerned for the spiritual condition and care of his people.

Pastors are not the whole answer to a healthy church. Apostolic, prophetic, teaching, and evangelistic leaders are also needed. But pastors can provide the care that will nourish the development of a broad range of gifts and ministries.

The church is growing worldwide, in spite of the assault by various philosophies and religions, with great persecution in some areas. If the harvest is to be conserved and new leaders cultivated, the entire church must focus on the real nature of pastoral care and how it can function to make the church healthy and powerful.

Pastoral leadership must go beyond maintenance and focus on building a victorious church. Pastoral leadership must also cause the church to focus on its mission to the entire earth.

Pastoral care without this purpose will produce self-centered Christians whose chief aim is to be mothered by God. If we really care, we will help Christians to live for a purpose beyond themselves, namely the kingdom of God that is filling the earth with his glory.

Other Books of Interest from Servant Books

Divine Appointments
Larry Tomczak

How you can step into the miraculous world of powerful, effective evangelism by allowing God to set up divine appointments for you to keep. *$5.95*

Every Day with Andrew Murray
Andrew Murray

Six months of devotional readings that can open you to the Holy Spirit's action to renew your life day by day. *$3.95*

Censorship: Evidence of Bias in Our Children's Textbooks
Paul C. Vitz

Are public school textbooks biased? Are they censored? This two-year study by Paul Vitz, funded by the National Institute of Education, reports that religion, family values, and certain political and economic positions have all been reliably omitted from children's textbooks. A handbook for parents, educators, and others who want to do something about it. *$6.95*

Available at your Christian bookstore or from
**Servant Publications • Dept. 209 • P.O. Box 7455
Ann Arbor, Michigan 48107**
Please include payment plus $.75 per book
for postage and handling
*Send for your FREE catalog of Christian
books, music, and cassettes.*